Studies  erience

A SENSE OF PRESENCE

A SENSE OF PRESENCE

The phenomenology of certain kinds of
visionary and ecstatic experience, based on
a thousand contemporary
first-hand accounts.

by

TIMOTHY BEARDSWORTH

The Religious Experience Research Unit
Manchester College, Oxford

© The Religious Experience Research Unit,
Manchester College, Oxford. 1977

ISBN 0 906165 00 8

20025994

201.1

We gratefully acknowledge permission from the following to quote copyright material:
Hamish Hamilton Ltd., Palinurus (Cyril Connolly), *The Unquiet Grave;* The Hogarth Press, *The Standard Edition of the Complete Psychological Works of Sigmund Freud,* Translated and Edited by James Strachey, Vol. 14; The Institute of Psychophysical Research, Oxford, Celia Green, *Out-of-the-Body Experiences;* Johnson Publications Ltd., John Custance, *Adventure into the Unconscious*; Methuen Children's Books (Text Copyright University Chest Oxford), Kenneth Grahame, *The Wind in the Willows;* Tavistock Publications Ltd., R. D. Laing, *The Divided Self.*

CONTENTS

NATURE OF THE ENQUIRY

The phenomena here described are the fruits (but only some of the fruits) of an enquiry into contemporary religious experience. They come from confidential, first-hand accounts supplied, in response to a request, between June 1969 and June 1970. The first thousand accounts received provide the data. The request was made by Professor Sir Alister Hardy, F.R.S., founder and first director of the Religious Experience Research Unit, Oxford. It was published first in religious journals — thirty, from as wide a variety of faiths and denominations as possible — later in newspapers — the Guardian, Times, Observer, Daily Mail, and certain overseas papers — and finally on radio and television. By far the most replies came in response to the newspaper appeal.

Sir Alister asked for accounts of a certain type of religious experience, for it did not seem practicable to study all kinds at once. He defined the type by means of quotations:

e.g. 1. "I find it best to live as if the soul of man were in communion with a superhuman force which makes for righteousness." — Beatrice Webb.

2. "There is that in the world, call it what you will, which responds to the confidence of those who trust it . . . Wherever there is a soul in darkness, obstruction or misery, there also is a Power which can help, deliver, illuminate and gladden that soul. This is the Helper of men . . . the God who is love." — L. P. Jacks.

3. "It is the common experience of man that he can draw on a power that makes for, and in its most typical form wills, righteousness, the sole condition being that a certain fear, a certain shyness and humility, accompany the effort to do so." — R. R. Marett.

There is an ambiguity about the phrase "religious experience", depending on how we take the word "experience". If we interpret it on the analogy of phrases like "interesting experience" or "harrowing experience", then we shall think in terms of episodes occurring at certain times and in certain places; we shall talk of "*a* religious experience" or "religious experience*s*". On the other hand, one can argue, as a contributor did, "Religious experience is not something to be tied down to definite times and places; it is *a way of looking at the world* (and oneself) which colours, or should colour, all one's thoughts and actions."

It was this second, dispositional type of experience that Sir Alister was chiefly concerned to investigate. However, his attempt to limit the scope of the enquiry seems to have had not the slightest effect on the response. Replies came in giving accounts of ecstatic and mystical episodes of every kind.

In this report I confine myself to accounts of these vivid or ecstatic episodes. You will find no sweeping explanations of them, whether reductionist (e.g. "It's all sex") or transcendental ("God moves in a mysterious way"). My approach is, in the jargon, "phenomenological", — i.e. concerned with each individual's exact description of his experience (assuming that he is telling the truth), regardless of whether what seemed to him to happen "really" happened or not. Indeed, the question of establishing whether something "really" happened can hardly arise in this field. It makes no sense to talk of overhearing the voice of God talking to somebody else (it is not that kind of "voice"); any more than talk of "the all-seeing eye of God" can give rise to questions about God's eyebrows.

You will find nothing in the way of statistical measurement here, and no inferences drawn from this biased sample about the incidence of the various kinds of experience in the population at large. Instead, the emphasis being on each individual's experience as he describes it, you will find a great deal of quotation, comparison and contrast. This attention to words, and to the phenomena as experienced will, I hope, yield a book that is interesting in itself, whether as bedside reading or as supplying data for students. What has struck me in reading these accounts is the candour with which the contributors set down their most intimate experiences. This has a salutary effect on the reader. As one looks, say, at passers-by in the street, it makes one tend to see them as each (like oneself) in his own particular predicament, reaching beyond himself for a meaning or a solution. And this seems to me a good thing to realise.

The episodes I shall quote involve "sensory"[1] phenomena — visions, voices, and the like. I classify the phenomena under separate heads according to the "sense" involved: (1) visual, (2) auditory, (3) tactile, (4) inward sensations[2]. There is also (5) the sense of a "presence", the feeling that someone is there, based on no sensory evidence at all. This feeling, I think, so far from being out on a limb, somehow underlies the other "sensory" categories.

This brings me to the method of reference. Within the five main categories just mentioned, different sub-categories are distinguished by letters of the alphabet; and within each sub-category, different individual examples by numbers. So 2b (1) will mean 2: auditory, b: guiding "voice", (1) particular example.

I refer to those who have submitted accounts as "contributors". Their accounts being confidential, no names are mentioned. Instead, before each quotation, I give the sex, marital status and age of the contributor (if known), and, in square brackets after it, his age at the time of the experience (if known). Thus —

M s 29: "..................................." [18]

Here M = male; m = married; w = widow or widower; F = female; s = single. Any other possibly relevant or interesting details about the contributor are added in brackets.

In a note, if more than one quotation is made from the same account, there is a cross-reference to the others. Thus —

= p. 55, 2b (1)

Except where otherwise noted, all italics are mine.

Introduction: Notes

1. I put "sensory" in inverted commas because, as normally used, it implies the existence of that which is sensed, and I am leaving this question open. Strictly, I should do the same for "visual", "auditory" and "tactile"; they too should be understood in this wider sense.
2. Smells I omit, since only four cases were reported — two nice (the scent of violets) and two nasty (the stench of death).

CHAPTER 1

VISUAL EXPERIENCE

I: a. VISIONS

Common enough in Biblical times[1], but nowadays out of fashion among the Christian orthodox. Eighty-nine contributors described visions; several said they had never told anyone before (not even wives or husbands) for fear of ridicule. Some described visions of a malign presence, whether indistinct —

e.g. (1) M m 52: "Twice in Egypt I had a sense of overpowering evil . . Both times it was the seeing awareness of a malign presence so *tangible* that it was endowed with *something like shape*. The effect was to make my limbs rigid and induce profuse sweating . . ."

— or clearly defined —

e.g. (2) M s 62: ". . . In the early part of last June one beautiful morning at dawn looking through the window I saw what looked to be a flying saucer — before I could get out of bed — from the size of an egg it moved at great speed to the window — an object the size of a large crab — with fearsome underpart which *watched me* at the only point to do so through the six inch curtain gap — I was *petrified* — even though I stared back — a set of valves pumped round the body which on going down another set took their place — I knew *it could tell what I was thinking* and its intense animosity only disappeared when I thought "Aye you from the spirit of my mother?", when it slowly rose, bent itself round the lintel and gradually went out of sight . . . It was a solid object (equally as frightening was its shadow on the opposite wall) . . . bright and overpowering . . . I had the *feeling of being engulfed* . . ."

— or else a wrathful presence —

e.g. (3) M m 81: "I remember omitting to say my bedside prayers one night and *imagined God was watching me* outside through the window. I was terrified (age about eight) and covered my head."[2]

But much more often the visions described were comforting — e.g. (4) F m 66 (U.S.A.): ". . . tiny lights (rays) came out of his *eyes*; as they neared me, they grew wider and wider and when they reached my body I was literally bathed in the light. It was *warm* . . . It made me feel wonderful . . ."

(5) M 64: ". . . As I threw my leg across the horse, the saddle slipped and I fell to the ground. I was unhurt, and my bowler hat saved my head. I landed on my back and at once found, to my concern, that my left foot was caught firmly in the stirrup; the fall had startled the mare, and she had twisted away from me, so my leg was stretched taut, and my foot bent back; I was lying partly in front of her . . . I remember how absolutely clear my brain was, as I considered the situation. I have never known such utter clarity of thought. It seemed that I must be facing very serious injury or death without a chance of being able to help myself. My thoughts went to my parents — both long dead — and to my Maker. Then a most astonishing thing happened. In my predicament, I became aware of a number of figures moving towards me. I could only see them in one direction, but I felt that they were all around me. When I first noticed them, they were perhaps 20 yards from me. There they all stopped and waited. Strangely, all my apprehension vanished, as I saw them. They brought me comfort, for it became certain to me that they were people who had known me in earlier days, who had known my danger and had come back to help me. I thought at once, "If I am to be killed, they have come to help me over, but if I am not to be killed, the mare will not move while I'm getting free". I remember no feeling of surprise at seeing these figures and the conclusions I came to seemed natural and certain. From then, on my elbows and back, I worked myself round until I was roughly at right angles to the mare's body, when my foot suddenly came free. As it did so, the figures vanished . . ."

Already we may notice something significant about visions — they are "effectively charged", that is, they characteristically induce strong emotion in the subject. Their effect may be comforting or frightening, awe-inspiring or enrapturing. Very often they occur at times of crisis or depression, bringing a dramatic change of mood —

e.g. (6) F s 59: "I was working in a hospital at Christchurch in Hampshire, living at home. I wasn't very efficient and was very unhappy at home. One night I had a vision of joy in the next world, expressed to me in a way I as a Catholic would understand — joy on the face of the Virgin Mary."

(7) F m 54: "A crisis arose when I decided I couldn't resolve the matter and simply asked Christ to 'take over'. I had an overwhelming feeling that he was in the room; he appeared larger than life-size . . ."

This affective relation between subject and apparition often results in a particular physical attitude or posture being adopted by the subject (cf. (3) above) — .

e.g. (8) F m 59: ". . . I felt impelled to *bow my head* . . . A sudden desire to look up and see for myself what I had been perceiving brought the experience to an abrupt end."

(9) F w (describing death of her husband): ". . . Two days later when his end was near, he suddenly *sat bolt upright* in bed, and almost *cowering* to the wall, and *shading his eyes,* said in awed tones and in fearfulness: "I see God — I see God in his power . . ."

The affectively neutral vision, described as it were by an interested but uninvolved spectator, is quite exceptional —

(10) F m: ". . . I distinctly saw my husband who had a very high I.Q. and a friend of his who is also brilliant, both wearing clear domes, helmet-shaped over their heads in order to protect their brains because all around them the earth was being tumulted by grey rocks and matter flying about and falling from the direction of the sky. The entire scene was dusty and grey. There was no sun or real daylight nor was it night-time or dusk at the time. Just a greyness that seemed present a long, long time. They were about to enter a restaurant . . ."

The affective relation is personal; i.e. it is a "second-person" relation ("I — You") between subject and apparition; the subject very often feels that he is *being watched* (whether disturbingly or reassuringly)[3], if not spoken to. Face[4] and facial expression feature prominently.

3

Often the vision occurs not *in vacuo*, but is suggested by something already there, such as a statue or portrait, which "comes to life"[5].

e.g. (11) F m 62: " . . . As I looked into the face of Washington, the stone face changed, he *looked down at us and smiled . . .*"

(12) F m 54: ". . . The portrait on the wall before me . . . the head *moved and inclined itself towards me . . .* and a *half-smile* . . . he spoke . . ."

(13) M 66: ". . . At Wells Cathedral there is, you may remember, a magnificent crucifix over the Chancel Arch. The procession entered the Cathedral to the hymn "Hail to the Lord's Annointed" . . . It seemed to me that the figure of Christ definitely *came to life* at this moment and *his presence seemed very near . . .*"

From these, that we should normally call visions, comes an insensible gradation to the following, (14) — (20), which we should hesitate to call visions, for they depend on imagination (14) or a "funny feeling" (of being watched, etc.), rather than actually "seeing things". But my point is that the difference is one of degree; the "affective relation" is at the heart of them both.

Patterns in the wall-paper may form "faces" —

(14) F m 59: ". . . Vivid impressions of quite distinctive *faces* always emerge from patterns on wall-paper, stains on ceiling; *faces* appear as I shut my eyes for sleep . . . I possess two crudely carved African heads which have pleased or sad *expressions* (depending on circumstances)."

In all these cases the subject enters into a new relationship with something in the environment. Something he sees suddenly becomes a "you", and he sees (and reacts to) it as "friendly", "hostile", "smiling" or whatever.

e.g. (15) F m 67: ". . . Feeling very despondent, I suddenly became aware of a great friendliness surrounding me. The sky, flowers, trees and even the grass was pulsing with friendliness . . ." [47][6]

(16) M 79 (Dr.): ". . . I was aware of Something 'within' and 'behind' the mere flowers: Something *aware of me* as I of It . . on one occasion, when there was a whole area of wild rock-roses, a pulsating halo over all, reminiscent of the 'burning'

4

bush . . . the impression is always that Something smiles and salutes and recognizes me, Something 'behind' or 'within' the flower . . ." [19 and after]

(17) M 63: ". . . The dew on the grass seemed to sparkle like irridescent jewels in the sunlight, and the shadows of the house and trees seemed *friendly* and *protective*. In the heart of the child that I was, there seemed suddenly to well up a deep overwhelming sense of gratitude, a sense of unending peace and security which seemed to be part of the beauty of the morning, the love and protection of my home and the sheer joy of being alive. I did not associate this with God, but I knew that in all this beauty was a friendliness, a protective and loving presence which included all that I had ever loved and yet was something much more . . ."

Not dissimilar are the following two examples where subject and object (in each case a tree) seem to 'reverse roles' —

(18) M 68: " . . . Quite suddenly, it seemed that I was *being looked at* very intently, and the look seemed to be coming from the tree, though whether it was the tree or the sky beyond which was acting I cannot say; it differed from my usual feeling . . . an aesthetic delight . . . my awareness of *my* looking . . . The other experience is one of *being myself looked at,* and of astonishment . . ." [35][7]

(19) F s 25: ". . . Around this time I spent a week at a Buddhist monastery in the Borders. While I was walking outside one day I felt the touch of the air on my face and the sound of the breeze in my ears. It suddenly came to me: This is God speaking to me — *it was as if I and the outside world changed places* . . . Later — during a walk in private gardens back in Edinburgh I was aware of a similar kind of experience with the trees. Again there was *reversal*: as I stood, running my hands over the tree bark in the twilight, *I* was the object and the tree *became the subject* . . ."

Compare this experience in early childhood —

(20) M 70 (Rev.): ". . . In 1908 or 1909, at a Sunday School Mission I was carried away emotionally and 'gave my heart to Jesus'. On the Monday morning I knew myself to be in a new world. The east wall of the Sunday School butted on to the playground of the playground of the village school.

During playtime *I felt strangely drawn to the wall.* I stroked it and felt I wanted to kiss it. I was mentally and emotionally 'uplifted' . . . Boys came and asked me to join in the usual playground games but I asked to be left alone . . ." [aged 8 or 9].

Visions may be of the familiar or unfamiliar. Of the former, by far the commonest kind described were cases where somebody recently dead "appeared" to be bereaved, usually to comfort or encourage them, usually someone who had been very close (especially husband, wife or parent) — [8]

e.g. (21) M 73 (U.S.A.): ". . . My mother passed away in May, 1921 . . . One night, about 1.30 a.m., I got out of bed and went to the bathroom. I will admit I had been sound asleep and was probably sleepy when I sat down in the bathroom with my head in my hands as you will please now try to visualize. I sat there looking at the floor, thinking of various things, when suddenly I became acutely conscious of someone or something in the hallway. The bathroom door was open, and I was gripped with great fear as *a bright golden light* appeared on the bathroom floor, and I feared to turn my head to look. I finally did, and there before me stood my mother. It is not possible for me to describe what I saw, but I know now, from *the expression in her eyes,* that she wanted me to know there is life after death . . ."

(22) M 70 (Rev.) [9]: ". . . Ever since my confirmation I had spent a long time in prayer every night before an 'altar' in my room. And on Friday nights, when I began my preparation for Sunday's Holy Communion I spent far longer than usual — often nearly an hour. I was about 18 (1918). One Friday night after a long time in prayer, I lay in bed with my eyes wide open wondering if God did intend me to be ordained or not (this was after the 'Little-Go' exam failure). I felt tears trickling down my cheeks. I said aloud: 'Oh God, what shall I do? If only I knew.' And then my father's face appeared over me. It seemed so real — as if I could have touched it. The only remarkable thing (to me) was that it was larger-than-life-size. His face was *very* large — like a close-up on a cinema screen. He smiled and said: "Stick it, Lad, stick it", and gave me another reassuring smile and vanished. This was a real experience. I turned over and cried myself to sleep with

sheer joy at having seen my father again. I had no doubts now . . ."

cf.   F w: ". . . There is no doubt in my mind now of survival, because of his expression . . ., wonder and joy written in his face as he smiled at me."

There was even one case of a dog "appearing" —

(23) F m 58: ". . . Our dog Judy died suddenly. Two nights later I was woken up somehow, and this is difficult to describe. I seemed to *slide out of myself*[10] and stand by the bed, looking forward and to the right. I saw a *warm glow*[11] with the dog standing there looking up at someone. I could only see the dog, but felt conscious of someone. It appeared that the dog was told to *look at me*. She saw me and curled up in pleasure; it seemed to me she was taken away then. However, as she walked away, she turned and looked at me again. That was the end."

Visions of the unfamiliar were chiefly of God (frightening or comforting), Christ (always comforting), more rarely of the devil (or some other evil and disturbing figure). In a sense these were not altogether unfamiliar, as the subject would have heard or read about them, though not "seen" them previously; he would at least be familiar with the concept.

But there were a few cases where the subject experienced totally strange, non-personal apparitions —

e.g. (24) ". . . Suddenly, I felt a great joyousness sweeping over me. I use the word sweeping, because this feeling seemed to do just that. I actually felt it as coming from my left and sweeping around and through me, completely engulfing me. I do not know how to describe it. It was not like a wind. But suddenly It was there and I felt it moved around and through me. Great joy was in it. Exaltation might be a better word. I looked up quickly, assuming that this feeling had swept through the congregation. I expected to see everyone ready to shout, for that was the way I felt. My head must have been turned slightly to the right, for as I looked up the persons across the aisle were the first ones I saw. They were calmly going ahead with their singing, obviously unaware of anything unusual. This puzzled me. Wonderingly I turned my head back to normal position and there, a few pews ahead of me and just above the heads of the congregation I saw the beginning of what was to be the most astonishing thing I have ever seen.

I saw movement in the air that was visible just as movement. That is, the air itself was in motion. In horizontal space about seventeen or eighteen inches long by about seven or eight inches high, the air was in motion. The lengthwise edges of this area were very smooth and even, but the ends were uneven as though broken or fading out. That is, this area appeared to be a fragment of a longer shaft. The movement was visible in the manner of 'dancing air' on a hot day. However, instead of the short, agitated movement of dancing air, this movement seemed graceful and unhurried . . . . ."[12]

In the next example, the subject "realised that it was God coming", but in a strange form (reminiscent of the previous example, but frightening, not joyful) —

(25) F m: ". . . I went to the church where I spent a great deal of time, since I played for the youth services on the organ and also practised piano in the church basement. This time I had decided that I would stay in the church over night, just to be doing it. I went to one of the social rooms where there was a couch and settled myself, hearing the preacher leave for home and knowing the church was now empty. After a bit as I sat, it was just beginning to lose some of the light, but the room was still very light, I began to observe without seeing anything, a circular movement start in the upper right hand corner of the room. The movement grew gradually louder and with it a roar (not audible) grew gradually louder. There was a tremendous feeling of an impersonal power entering the room, a power that belonged here and was oblivious of me. By the time the movement had reached halfway across the room and the roar had gathered a power to go with it, I was so frightened I realized that this was God coming, and nothing could stand in His way, and that I was utterly unprepared to meet Him and utterly unworthy and if I stayed I would likely lose my mind, and I got up and ran out of the church . . ."[13]

Two contributors "saw" writing —[14]

(26) F m 32: ". . . In early May of 1968 I awoke suddenly. I saw a vision very clearly against the dark night. It was all in

8

symbols and I still don't understand the meaning of it. However, I had no difficulty in understanding the *feeling* surrounding this vision: take the words CALM, GOOD and PERFECT and make them into one word, multiplying its meaning by 100. But how can one adequately describe a feeling, especially when there is as yet no word for it? . . ."

(27) F m: ". . . This posed so many problems, financial and otherwise, that I turned to God for a solution. I knelt on the floor with my arms resting on the seat of a big, over-stuffed, tweedy type chair. As I opened my eyes, I beheld in cursive writing, on the back of that chair, "Missouri, receive you.' (My prayerful question had been: 'Should we move to Missouri?' That is where Milton was born). I stared in disbelief, shook my head and moved my eyes to another sort of chair only to see the same message there. This happened a third time. On the strength of this, and because of my faith, we prepared for the move . . ."

But much more often the vision was of a "speaking" apparition (cf. (22) above). Indeed these were nearly as common as "silent" visions. (Cases where voices alone were "heard", and nothing "seen" I discuss later under 2 "auditory".)

Apparitions were sometimes bathed in a "warm glow" or "dazzling light",[15] as in (4) and (23) above. Compare also (9), ("shading his eyes") —

e.g. (28) M m 66: ". . . Awaking at about 4.0 p.m., I became aware of a fragrant perfume and a tremendous feeling of power,[16] and looking through the bottom of the net at the end of my bed I was amazed to see a beautiful figure *shrouded in a tremendous light*. I could not believe in the reality of this phenomenon at first and rubbed my eyes to ensure that this was an experience in the realm of reality. Pulling up the mosquito net I sat upon the side of the bed and for a short time gazed at the wonderful 'being' just beyond the end of my bed. Standing upon my feet I suddenly ran towards the bottom of the bed crying out words of endearment, but the figure disappeared, but the wonderful fragrance remained . . . . . ."

(29) F m 80: ". . . Not only the sky but the whole air seemed full of dazzling light . . ."

(30) F m 74: ". . . There was a glow of light by the wardrobe and standing in front of it was Christ. I fully opened my eyes in amazement and knew that I must be dreaming. But when He spoke in a wonderfully comforting and reassuring voice, I knew He was there. He just said, with real compassion in his voice, 'You will see your son in his profession.' He then raised his right hand in blessing and the glow of light and Christ gradually disappeared . . ."

(31) F 81: ". . . It was in the night and I was lying awake when suddenly I saw a small intensely bright light in the room which grew until it assumed the proportions of a man. Yet it was not a human figure that I saw but a great luminosity which brought me a wonderful calm and deep content. There was communication but not by audible word or visual sign. It was an assurance and an inspiration which revealed to me that I had a mission, and as the light faded I knew that one day I must found a centre where teachers and students would find their inspiration to create beauty and thus be drawn into the perfection of God. This vision remained clear throughout the years and became the mainspring of my enthusiasm and the secret of the response it drew from others . . ."

Many contributors wrote simply of "seeing" light, a light, or lights, without any accompanying apparition. ((31) borders on this). These cases I discuss separately below (1b and c), as with "voices" unaccompanied by vision (2a and b).

As for the verbs used by contributors to introduce their experiences, they range from the bald, firm "I knew" (30), or "I saw", (2) and (7), (or, more high-flown, "I beheld" (27)) to expressions less certain and definite: e.g. "It seemed that..." (18) "I imagined . . ." (i.e. I thought I saw) (3); "I began to observe without seeing anything" (25); "I felt an awareness of"; "I seemed to feel rather than to see"; "I had a strong feeling that"; " 'I saw' " (in quotes).

The subject's own state at the time ranges from the active and wide-awake ("When I was hanging up washing" (29); "I was ironing in the kitchen" (8); "The saddle slipped and I fell to the ground" (5)) to the sleepy and near dreaming ("I will admit I had been sound asleep, and probably sleepy when I sat down in the bath-room" (21); "Awakening about 4 p.m." (28); "I awoke suddenly . . ." (26); "I fully opened my eyes in amazement and knew that I must be dreaming, but . . ." (30)). Also, of course, the experience comes while praying ("I simply asked Christ to take over" (7); "I turned to God for a solution" (27)).

Chapter 1: a: Notes

1. See, for example, St. Luke, Chapter 1, where "the angel of the Lord" appears to Zacharias ("Fear not . . . thy prayer is heard"), to Mary ("Fear not . . . thou hast found favour") and to the shepherds ("Fear not . . . I bring you good tidings").

2. cf. another contributor, F s 60: "I often think of God telling Moses to hide his face until He had gone by, for nobody could look upon I AM'S face without being destroyed". (cf. the Medusa legend).

3. cf. (2), (3) & (4) above; also —
   F m 44: ". . . In the summer of August 1966, around 11 p.m., my family had gone to bed so I decided to read for a while. I had a strong feeling someone was *watching me* . . ." (Then she describes her vision).

   and F m: ". . . I felt two eyes burning right into me — so penetrating that I could not bear to look at them — then they were gone . . ."

4. cf. "The Lord lift up the light of his countenance upon you"; "The Lord make his face to shine upon you", etc. — Numbers 7: 25-6.

5. Primitive people often believe in a magical identity between image and living original.

6. cf. Housman:
   "In my own shire, if I was sad,
   Homely comforters I had;
   The earth, because my heart was sore,
   Sorrowed, for the child she bore;
   And standing hills, long to remain,
   Shared their short-lived comrade's pain."
   or (Ronald Searle's Fotherington-Thomas: "Hello, clouds! Hello, sky!" etc.).

7. These "reversals" perhaps throw light on autoscopic experiences (seeing one's own body from the outside); see 1e below.

8. cf. St. Luke (after the crucifixion): "And as they thus spoke, Jesus himself stood in the midst of them and saith unto them: 'Peace be unto you!' But they were terrified and affrighted, and supposed they had seen a ghost." (24: 36-37)
   It is remarkable how common this experience is today. A

Welsh G.P. (W. D. Rees, B.M.J. Oct. 1971, 4, 37-41), taking as a cross-section of the community those who attended his surgery, found that *45%* of the widows and widowers had experienced it at least once — (many of them of non-Celtic stock). Figures for men were about the same as for women. (For visions and voices in general, not just to do with the departed, our own figures for women were higher than for men. Twice as many women as men wrote in altogether, but more than three times as many of the accounts of visions and voices were from women.)

9. = (20) above.

10. cf. "Out-of-the-body" experiences, 1e below.

11. cf. (4), (9), (21), (28) — (31); also "Illumination" 1b below, and "A light or lights" 1c below.

12. In Latin ("spiritus"), Greek ("pneuma") and many other languages (e.g. Nuer "kwoth"), the word for "Spirit" also means "breath".

13. cf. *Acts of the Apostles*: "And suddenly there came a sound from heaven as of a rushing mighty wind, and it filled the house where they were sitting." (2: 1-2).

14. cf. Belshazzar's experience while feasting: "Suddenly there appeared the fingers of a human hand writing on the plaster of the palace wall." (Daniel, 5: 5)

15. a. cf. Note 4 above: (". . . make his face to *shine* upon you" "lift up the *light* of his countenance") and St. Luke ("the glory of the Lord *shone* round about them"). This phenomenon occurs very frequently in the Bible, cf. Saul's blinding vision on the way to Damascus (*Acts of the Apostles* 10: 3-4): "And as he journeyed, he came to Damascus: and suddenly there shone round him a *light* from heaven, and he fell to the earth, and heard a voice saying . . ."

    b. Experiments of E. Hess show that the pupil becomes enlarged when looking at anything interesting or attractive, so admitting more light to the eye. Hence "dazzling' beauty, etc. may be more than just a metaphor.

16. The "fragrant perfume" is unusual. As I have said, only four out of the first thousand contributors report olfactory sensations. But the feeling of power is reported by several other contributors

— cf. (25) "a tremendous feeling of an impersonal *power* entering the room . . .", (9) "I see God in his *power*." (8) (continued) ". . . Glancing out of the window at the beauty of the trees I suddenly became aware of an upsurge of *power* as of the growth fluid in and among them and an awareness of the all-pervading colour green. Immediately afterwards this uprush was followed by a descending sweep of *power* flooding into the room till I was overwhelmed by it entirely . . ."

I: b. ILLUMINATION OF SURROUNDINGS (LATIN "LUMEN")

You could call this (like (c) below) a particular kind of vision. I think it worth distinguishing at least as an interesting and common sub-class. We have already met with apparitions accompanied by light (pp. 6ff. above). Light alone may be tackled under two heads: (1) light diffused all around[1], which I deal with now, calling it "illumination of surroundings" — though this omits the important fact that some contributors "felt" it "within", as well as "seeing" it around them; (2) by contrast, a particular light or lights (dealt with under (c) below).

Twenty contributors described experiences of "illumination" (unaccompanied by voices or apparitions). Often the experience followed a period of depression —

e.g. (1) M 56: ". . . My work suffered, a period of acute lack of confidence and withdrawal followed, and my appointment was terminated as the work of the research station folded up. The experience which came as a liberation from the state described above must have been in the spring of 1940, my age then being 26. I think I must have been in the habit of praying formally for enlightenment in what had become darkness. The experience itself was one of an amazing bright light in the form of *an inward illumination, not of a kind detectable by eye,* but one was seeing things and people in a way not previously experienced. They were seen *lit up* as though in a glow. Although this event could be pinpointed almost to the day and has never been repeated, one's whole being was suffused . . . a state of wellbeing is a tame way of describing the response. One's thinking was elevated to an exalted plane, no evil was apparent, only pristine freshness and warmth . . ."

(2) M: ". . . For weeks I had been in heavy depression and sadness; as a conscientious objector and strongly opposed to war I could feel the hopeless stupidity of it all . . . Suddenly everything became crystal clear, clearer, more definite than anything in normal existence. There was also an amazing 'knowingness' rather than knowledgeableness,

that is, I knew, not by application to study, but because it was in my mind from the beginning and had so existed as an attribute, a primary possession . . . Why, the thought kept running in my mind, in our everyday life we are asleep, drugged as under a spell; eyes unseeing and minds clogged, ears stone deaf and senses completely dulled with the heavy stupor of day-to-day existence and the senseless round of useless duties, routine and habits . . . I seemed to be aware of a *radiance surrounding me,* everywhere it penetrated; it was a light that seemed to have *no visible source,* no point of emanation, but it was found, seen and felt everywhere. I was my own questioner and answerer, and fast as the questions came, out trundled the answer, so easy to comprehend and always, always right, the only possible answer. In that state, death was a laughing impossibility, the thought of death — well, it was too absurd to consider, even for one moment. Death was and is not. I longed, completely and fully, to stay in that state forever, but I felt my earth-bound body slowly pulling me back to 'reality'. I tried desperately to hold on to the vision, for I knew the pangs of anguish with the thought of returning to the world, the bitterness, the loneliness, the drabness, the hate and the envy of life. I can only describe it as the feeling of an angel banished from the courts of light. All effort was unavailing. I became aware that my head was resting against the side of the horizontal storage tank, and I was standing relaxed, gazing towards the windows facing the road, and through which the morning light shone. There was absolute silence everywhere (though hundreds of people were, in fact, round about . . . Then gradually, very faint at first and then with increasing sound I heard moving machinery; the wheels were revolving; G . . . .was moving; the pan of the scale tipped down. All this happened on the third floor of the Kersal Vale, Manchester, factory of Cussons, Sons & Co. The memory was intense for several years and I wrote it down then."

— or bereavement —

e.g. (3)   F s 85: ". . . I remember very clearly an experience I had when I was 28. I had had news of the death of a sister whom I loved very much and my grief was deepened by the fear that I might have prevented her from 'finding salvation'. I was lying in bed, feeling extremely miserable and hopeless and cold. Suddenly my heart lifted and I felt real warmth flow through me and a golden light around me . . ."

(4)   M 44 (Rev.): ". . . Gradually I became aware that my wife would not survive. Probably I deduced this from the bland pap and evasions that were all I could elicit by my questions concerning her welfare. I do not now remember whether it was before or after her death that an incredible sense of security crept over me. It was a sense of *being loved* and cherished. I heard nothing, yet it was as if I were surrounded by golden light and as if I only had to reach out my hand to touch God himself who was so surrounding me with his compassion. Later a Surgeon Captain remarked upon my euphoria while in hospital and I had no objection to make to his term. I think, nevertheless, that my experience was not wholly subjective for many people sensed something in my cabin and the rumour that something special was happening got around the Fleet. Months later, moreover, a Scottish Medical Officer — considerably the worse for drink — demanded that I should 'show him God'. He said, 'You've got Him. I know it. He was in your cabin in the hospital. Day after day I felt him there'. I am certain that at no time had I mentioned my feeling to him . . ."

Sometimes the experience occurred at a time of crisis — e.g. (5)   F m: ". . . My marriage had reached a critical period and I was in a somewhat despairing position . . . the time was very late at night or very early morning; the physical darkness in the room matched the inner darkness of my mood. I came to a decision which I thought would be the best for all of us when the room was filled with light of a quality unknown to me before . . ."

(6)   F m 63: ". . . Four months ago I had to go into hospital to have a major operation, and, with no experience of such things, I was extremely apprehensive. As I lay in bed alone (in a private room) waiting to be taken off to unknown horrors, I prayed for help and was reading the 23rd Psalm to myself when suddenly *I felt something in the room*[2], but with no visible presence, except that I thought it became *a little lighter*. Immediately I felt secure and unafraid and waited quite calmly to be fetched for the operation . . ."

17

As one would expect, it often happened in the dark (as in (5) above) —

e.g. (7) F m: ". . . It seemed to me I had been searching for peace, and at last I had found it. After putting my light out and getting into bed, my bedroom was *strangely lit*, there were no stars nor a moon — I do not remember sleeping that night. The Glory of the Lord[3] was with me. It was as if I had been blind and now I could see the meaning of God's purpose for me . . .".

And often in answer to prayer, whether for oneself (cf. (1) and (6) above) —

e.g. (8) M: ". . . On the first night, I knelt to say my prayers which I had now made a constant practice, I was aware of a glowing light which seemed to envelope me and which was accompanied by a sense of warmth all round me . . . "

(9) F m 45: ". . . I awoke in the middle of the night, still burdened with anxiety, and prayed, using the words of the hymn,

　　　Thou Whose Almighty Word
　　　Chaos and darkness heard . . .
　　　Let there be light . . .

I lay in bed, conscious of being absolutely wide awake. The bedroom seemed to be filled with an atmosphere of peace and light (though it was still dark) which was *almost tangible . . .*"[4]

— Or for another —

e.g. (10) F s 78: ". . . A nephew of mine was very difficult — he would not work in School and was sent to a Detention Centre for stealing — I prayed for him constantly and one night while praying I became enveloped in a warm orange-coloured glow and received a feeling that all would be well with him.. . . . ."

But it also happened in daylight, particularly in connection with natural beauty —

e.g. (11) M 78: ". . . When I was about 8 years old we were living in the country. At the foot of our garden was a very old large pear tree, which at the time was crammed with white blossom and at its summit a blackbird was singing, while beyond the tree a meadow sloped up to a marvellous sunrise. As I looked at this someone or something said to me 'That is beautiful' and immediately the whole scene *lit up* as though a bright light had been turned on irradiating everything. The meadow was a more vivid green, the pear tree glowed and the blackbird's song was more loud and sweet. A curious thrill ran down my spine . . ."[5]

(12) F m 51: ". . . There was a mysterious presence in nature and sometimes met within the communion and in praying by oneself, which was my greatest delight, especially when as happened from time to time, *nature became lit up from inside* with something that came from beyond itself (or seemed to do so to me) . . ."

And also in less favourable surroundings —

e.g. (13) M m 74 (after the spiritual healing of his crippled daughter): ". . . The dirtiest streets and the dullest correspondence 'glowed' . . ."

One contributor described an experience that occurred in a crowded railway carriage —

(14) M 60 (Rev): ". . . Vauxhall Station on a murky November Saturday evening is not the setting one would choose for a revelation of God! I was a young theological student aged19, being sent from Richmond Theological College (London University) to take the services somewhere — I cannot remember where — for some minister in a Greater London Church who had fallen ill. The third class compartment was full. I cannot remember any particular thought processes which may have led up to the great moment. For a few seconds only, I suppose, the whole compartment was filled with light. This is the only way I know in which to describe the moment, for there was nothing to see at all. I felt caught up into some tremendous sense of being within a loving, triumphant and shining purpose. I never felt more humble. I never felt more exalted. A most curious but overwhelming sense possessed me and filled me with ecstasy. I felt that all was well for all mankind — how poor the words seem! The word 'well' is so poverty stricken. All men were heirs. My puny message if I passed my exams and qualified as a minister would contribute only an infinitesimal drop to the ocean of love and truth which God wanted men to enjoy, but

my message was of the same *nature* as that ocean. I was right to want to be a minister. I had wanted to be a doctor and the conflict had been intense, but in that hour I knew the ministry was the right path for me. For me it was right, right, right . . an indescribable joy possessed me . . ."

For two others the experience occurred while doing housework (cf. 1a (8) above: "One morning . . . I was ironing in the kitchen . . . then it suddenly happened . . .").

(15) M s 55: ". . . One lunch time I had been helping to dry dishes after the meal, and was standing before the open drawer of the sideboard putting knives and forks away. I was not thinking of anything, apart from vague attention to the job I was doing. Suddenly, without warning, I was flooded with the most intense blue-white light I have ever seen. Words can never adequately nor remotely touch the depth of this experience. It was like looking into the face of the sun, magnified several times in its light-intensity. It would be truer to say that I lost all sense of self in a total immersion in Light. But more 'real' than the Light itself was the unbearable ecstasy that accompanied it. All sense of time or self disappeared, yet it could only have been a fraction of a second. I knew only a sense of infinite dimension, and a knowledge that this was the Spirit of God Almighty, which was the hidden Life-Light-Love in all men, all life and all creation. I knew that nothing existed apart from this Spirit. It was infinite Love, Peace, Law, Power, Creation and the Ultimate Truth and Perfection. It was all Wisdom, Tolerance, Understanding and Eternal Life for all people. I also knew that had I been suffering from any so-called incurable disease whatsoever, I would have become instantly whole. Then after the fraction of a second — I became myself again, still standing beside the open drawer putting knives and forks away. That one moment was and remains the most vital moment of my life, for there has never been a repetition. But out of it was born the Mission to which I have for many years dedicated my life . . ."

(16) F m 48: ". . . A year ago while going about my normal duties as a housewife, I paused for a moment to see whether my mind was free from all thought about something which had caused me a great deal of unhappiness and pain. My mind

was perfectly controlled and I was just about to give myself a pat on the back and a 'well-done old girl' when — my vision was completely blocked out and light seemed all about my head — not the daylight but a light in my mind and around — I could as it were feel the walls of my head crumbling down. I cannot explain the degree of light; there is nothing to compare with it. I seemed to *become* this light and consciousness of my personal self seemed to be held very faintly and of no consequence. How this light was left behind or how I came out of it, I do not know... As quickly as I had merged into light, so once more I was returned to my duties . . ."

For one the experience was induced by "transcendental meditation" —

(17) F s: ". . . The effect was immediate and bewildering from the first meditation . . . Through all the objects in the room glowed a *radiance* . . ."

Another had been trying to help someone in difficulties —

(18) F s 19 (Oxford undergraduate): ". . . Then, the room seemed all of a sudden filled with light, a whitish light which was, nonetheless, warm. It seemed to be both in the room and within me. Although 'it' was obviously outside me, it was also part of me, yet a part which has no physical location: it was united completely with a region of my mind. The curious thing is that I *felt* the light. Although my eyes were open, the perception of the light was an *interior* perception. I continued to see everything in the room quite clearly, but all the objects were lit up by this interior light . . ."

— The experience was repeated a few weeks later —

". . . The whole thing lasted from 1055 p.m. until midnight. This time the outstanding feature was the change in perception. My eyes felt as though they were open very wide. The room was very bright and everything in it was shining . . . As in the first experience, I felt that my perception was not wholly visual, that, once again, I was 'seeing' with part of my mind . . ."

For most contributors the light was outside them, and all around them — favourite words are "surrounded by", "enveloped by", "around me". Thus —

(2) "A radiance surrounding me, everywhere it penetrated; it

21

was a light that seemed to have no visible source, no point of emanation, but it was found, seen and felt everywhere . . ."

(3)   ". . . A golden light around me . . ."

(4)   ". . . Surrounded by golden light . . ."

(5)   ". . . The room was filled with light of a quality unknown to me before . . ."

(6)   ". . . It became a little lighter . . ."

(7)   ". . . My bedroom was strangely lit . . ."

(8)   ". . . A glowing light which seemed to envelop me . . ."

(9)   ". . . I became enveloped in a warm orange-coloured glow. . ."

(10) ". . . The whole scene lit up as though a bright light had been turned on irradiating everything . . ."

(11) ". . . Intense light all around . . ."

(12) ". . . Nature became lit up from inside with something that came from beyond itself (or seemed to do so to me) . . ."

(13) ". . . Streets . . . correspondence 'glowed' . . ."

(14) ". . . The whole compartment was filled with light . . ."

(17) ". . . Through all the objects of the room glowed a radiance . . . . ."

But for some contributors the light seemed to be *inside* them as well as out —

(1)   ". . . An amazing bright light in the form of an *inward* illumination, not of a kind detectable by eye, but one was seeing things and people in a way not previously experienced. They were lit up as though in a glow . . . one's whole being was suffused . . ."

(15) ". . . I was flooded with the most intense blue-white light. It was like looking into the face of the sun, magnified several times in its intensity. It would be truer to say that I lost *all sense of self* in a total immersion in Light . . ."

(16) ". . . My vision was completely blocked out and light seemed all round my head — not the daylight but a light in my mind and around — I could, as it were, feel the walls of my head

crumbling down . . . I seemed to *become* this light and consciousness of my personal self seemed to be held very faintly and of no consequence."

(18) ". . . It seemed to be both in the room and within me. Although 'it' was obviously outside me, it was also part of me, yet a part which has no physical location: it was united completely with a region of my mind. The curious thing is that I *felt* the light. Although my eyes were open, the perception of the light was an *interior* perception . . ."

Words favoured for describing the light itself were — "radiance", "golden" (very often), "silver" (once only), "of a quality unknown to me before", "strange", "glowing", "warm orange-coloured glow", "bright", "intense", "amazing", "whitish, nonetheless warm".

One contributor described it as "smiling" —

(19) F m: ". . . I have seen it and would have to say that it smiles. And how can light smile? . . ."

But the description is not so strange. We talk of a "warm" light (indeed this is the epithet most commonly used here) and of a "warm" smile (or "radiant" smile), presumably because it induces (as well as expressing) feelings of warmth; so "smiling" light seems not inappropriate (cf. "Hail, smiling morn"). The question remains, just how far is it metaphorical?[6]

Affective States

This brings us to the affective reaction that the light elicits.

(1) ". . . a state of well-being is a tame way of describing the response . . ."

(2) ". . . In that state, death was a laughing impossibility . . ."

(3) ". . . My heart lifted and I felt real warmth flow through me . . ."

(4) ". . . It was as if I only had to reach out my hand to touch God himself who was so surrounding me with his compassion. . . .
. . ."

23

(6) ". . . Immediately I felt secure and unafraid . . ."

(7) ". . . It seemed to me I had been searching for peace, and at last I had found it."

(8) ". . . accompanied by a sense of warmth all around me."

(9) ". . . a feeling that all would be well . . ."

(11) ". . . a sense of warmth and glow, of utter contentment. . ."

(12) ". . . my greatest delight . . ."

(14) ". . . filled me with ecstasy . . . I felt that all was well for mankind . . . an indescribable joy possessed me . . ."

(15) ". . . More 'real' than the light itself was the unbearable ecstasy that accompanied it. All sense of time or self disappeared . . ."

(17) ". . . a feeling of absolute bliss . . ."

(18) ". . . As soon as I perceived this light, I felt great joy and peace; I wanted to worship the force which was manifesting itself in such an inexpressible way and which had come to comfort us in answer to our searching . . ."

Cognitive States

Apart from the emotions accompanying the experience, there is the cognitive state —

cf. (1) "One's *thinking* was elevated to an exalted plane . . ."

(2) "Suddenly everything became crystal clear, clearer, more definite than anything in normal existence. There was also an amazing 'knowingness' rather than knowledgeableness, that is, I *knew*, not by application to study, but because it was in my mind from the beginning . . . I was my own questioner and answerer, and fast as the questions came, out trundled the answer, so easy to comprehend and always, always right, the only possible answer . . ."

(7) ". . . It was as if I had been blind and now I could see the *meaning* of God's *purpose* for me . . ."

(14) ". . . I felt caught up into some tremendous sense of being

within a loving, triumphant and shining purpose . . . I was *right* to want to be a minister . . . For me it was right, right, right . . ."

(15) ". . . I *knew* . . . a sense of infinite dimension, and a *knowledge* that this was the Spirit of God . . . I *knew* that nothing existed apart from this Spirit . . . I also *knew* that . . ."

(17) ". . . All problems dissolved, or rather, there were no problems . . ."

(18) ". . . It ended with an indescribable feeling of strength, *certainty* and great serenity . . ."

Duration

How long did it last? The length of time varied from "a few seconds only (14), "a fraction of a second" (15), to "over an hour" (18). The after-effects sometimes persisted for weeks — e.g. (18) (who writes with great precision): "For at least a fortnight[7] afterwards I continued to perceive everything about me, both inside buildings and outside, with increased intensity"; (20) (in more high-flown language): "Re-enclosed again in dimness, this radiance still gleams", (11a): ". . . an aftermath remained and continued for several weeks. It was a sense of warmth and glow".

After-effects

As to the *effect* of the experience on the subject's subsequent way of life, for some it was "lasting"; "I became a different person"; "permanently changed my life and character", etc. But for the man who remembered it longest (11a) "gradually the memory became just a happy memory. I do not recall any marked ethical or other results". The most remarkable effect was on (15) — a prosperous business man who thereupon gave it all up and devoted himself entirely to faith-healing, with marked success: "That one moment was, and remains, the most vital moment of my life".

Language

How literal or metaphorical are the contributors' accounts? As before, we may consider the exact words each uses to introduce his experience. First, the qualified or subjective assertion —

(1) "Illumination, *not of a kind detectable by eye* . . . as though in a glow . . ."

(2) ". . . I *seemed* to be aware of . . ."

(3) ". . . I *felt* a golden light . . ."

(4) ". . . I saw nothing, yet *it was as if* . . ."

(6) ". . . I thought it became a little lighter . . ."

(8) ". . . *Seemed* to envelop me . . ."

(10) ". . . As *though* a bright light had been turned on . . ."

(13) ". . . 'Glowed' . . ." (in inverted commas).

(14) ". . . This is the only way I know in which to describe the moment, for there was nothing to *see* at all . . ."

(16) ". . . Light *seemed* all about my head . . ."

(18) ". . . The room *seemed* . . . It *seemed* to be . . . I *felt* the light . . . an *interior* perception . . ."

(21) F 80: ". . . It *seemed* to me . . . And I was aware I seemed to *feel* rather than to see . . ."

On the other hand, there were several plain, unqualified, quasi-factual accounts —

e.g. (5) ". . . The room was filled with light . . ."

— factual enough, but she adds, "of a quality unknown to me before".

cf. (7) ". . . My bedroom was strangely lit . . ."

(10) ". . . I became enveloped . . ."

(11a) ". . . I was suddenly acutely aware of . . ."

(12) ". . . Nature became lit up . . ."

26

(15) ". . . I was flooded . . ."

(17) ". . . Through all the objects in the room glowed a radiance . . ."

It is worth noting the extensive use made of paradox by some contributors, in attempting to describe what so many of them call "indescribable", "ineffable",[8] etc.

e.g. (1) ". . . Illumination not detectable by eye . . ."
(cf. 1a (25) above. "I saw without observing . . . heard without hearing . . .").

(14) ". . . I never felt more humble. I never felt more exalted . . ."

(18) ". . . timeless moment . . . and although 'it' (the light) was obviously outside me, it was also part of me, yet a part which has no physical location . . . I *felt* the light . . ."

(19) ". . . it (the light) smiles . . ."

Lastly, though I have lumped these experiences of "illumination" together, we must not overlook a basic distinction: for some it was a deeply moving experience, but impersonal, for others it was a meeting, an affective relation with a "You" (like the visions in 1a). Thus (1) and (2) are impersonal; — there is the light, the state of well-being, the exalted thinking, the feeling of knowing all the answers — very similar, in fact to another impersonal type of ecstatic experience, the feeling of oneness with one's surroundings, — 1d below. (11) too is impersonal — there is the light, the thrill, the enhanced beauty of the scene — but it has more in common with 1f — the experience of transformation of one's surroundings. On the other hand (4) and (6), with their sense of being loved and feeling that "God himself" (4) or "something" (6) was in the room comforting them, could not be more personal. And the same applies to those for whom the light was "smiling", "full of forgiveness", and "a focal point of wonderful compassion and understanding."

Chapter 1: b: Notes

1. William James, *The Varieties of Religious Experience,* (Longmans, Green, London, 1903), pp. 251-3, gives a number of good examples, borrowed from Starbuck; he calls these luminous phenomena "photisms".

2. cf. (4) ". . . people sensed something in my cabin . . ."

3. "*Glory* of the Lord"; we tend to think of glory as meaning no more than "fame". But experiences like this suggest that in the Bible it meant something that is *seen* in some fairly literal sense of the word "see", and the references to it there are not just vaguely metaphorical; cf. "the glory of the Lord shone around", and the Te Deum: "Pleni sunt coeli et terra maiestate gloriae tuae" — Nicetas is here describing something that he himself has been aware of in some quasi-visual way — i.e. something extended in space (cf. "pleni") filling the whole of his visual field. We may recall the Jews' doctrine of "shechinah", concerning the Holy of Holies. (And cf. also Wordsworth's account of his childhood world — "apparell'd in celestial light . . . The glory and the freshness of a dream").

4. cf. 1a (1) ". . . a malign presence so tangible . . ." But experiences of actually "touching" something are much rarer than experiences of being "touched": see Chapter 3.

5. See 1f below, transformation of surroundings. The vivid recollection of an event in early childhood (in this case seventy years earlier) is not uncommon among contributors, such is the impact of this kind of experience — cf. (11a) M 90 (Rev), recalling something that happened at his prep school: "As I was on my knees during the compulsory minutes that obtained during our arrival in the dormitory, suddenly, as I knelt (as was customary, but for most of us perfunctory) I was suddenly acutely aware of *intense light* all around. I recall looking through my fingers at the others still kneeling at their bedsides all around me, to see if they had noticed anything. But nothing suggested this — chatting as usual then and later as we undressed and got into bed. I also settled down in bed but was fully aware that an aftermath remained and continued for several weeks. It was a sense of warmth and glow, of utter contentment mixed with an expectancy and hope that the experience might be repeated. No

repeat of it came and gradually the memory became just a happy memory. I do not recall any marked ethical or other results..."[10]

6. Other examples: F m 63: ". . . Spoke in rather a shallow way of Christ. Later feeling of guilt. Light filled the room. *The Light was full of forgiveness.* Felt I had been taught how to forgive. I worshipped . . ."

   F w: ". . . Golden light which seemed to have a 'focal point' of wonderful compassion and understanding . . ."

   cf. also 1a (31): ". . . it assumed the proportions of a man, yet it was not a human figure that I saw but a great luminosity which brought me a wonderful calm and a deep content . . ."

7. cf. 1a (8): ". . . The pervading sense of well-being which followed lasted in an intense form *for about two weeks*, during which time I was 'walking on air'. Everything assumed an aura of beauty and sparkle which I could only liken to the exhilaration a lover must experience when in the realms of great happiness in knowing he loves and is loved in return . . ." (but the experience itself "could not have lasted for more than three or four seconds").

8. e.g. (15) ". . . Words can never adequately nor remotely touch the depth of this experience . . ."

   (16) " . . . I cannot explain the degree of light; there is nothing to compare it with . . ."

   — Note that for both these contributors there was an experience of *unity* ("I lost all sense of self in a total immersion in the light" (15), "I seemed to become this light" (16)). Language cannot remotely convey this experience because its functioning presupposes a world of discrete, particular objects identifiable and reidentifiable, and above all a distinction between subject and object ("I here" and "that there") which is here temporarily dissolved in immediate "preobjective" experience. See 1d below.

I: c. A LIGHT OR LIGHTS (LATIN "LUX")

Thirty-two contributors described experiences of seeing a light or lights.[1]
For six of them the experience was preceded by a period of difficulty or depression —

e.g. (1) F m 71: ". . . During the night of September 9th 1954, I awoke and looking out of my window saw what I took to be a luminous star which gradually came nearer, and appeared as a soft slightly blurred white light. I was seized with violent trembling, but had no fear. I knew that what I felt was great awe. This was followed by a sense of overwhelming love coming to me, and going out from me, then of great compassion from this Outer Presence. After that I had a sense of overpowering peace, and indescribable happiness. I remember saying to myself 'This is no dream, I am wide awake, and experiencing it with my whole self'. I remain convinced of this. I thought I heard a slight, whirring noise near me, as the light faded and disappeared, but this may have been imagined.

I awoke in the morning with a feeling of having been transformed, and in the days that followed, I had a very much clearer sense of my identity, saw people more clearly and things in a different way. Certainty about what I must do at that juncture of my life suddenly came to me. The experience came *after a period of emotional and mental upheaval,* and an appeal for help from outside, although for many years I had ceased to pray.

The desire to pray, however, now grew daily, and I have kept up the habit ever since . . . The sequence of the sensations described have remained very clear, i.e. Awe, Love, Compassion and Peace — in that order. I have never since doubted the existence of a Supreme Power, nor the power of prayer, nor lost a sense of eternity . . ."

(2) M 61 (Rev): ". . . In utter disillusionment with self and church, I came to 'the end of my tether'. *In a state of intense inner wretchedness,* of such intensity that my mind seemed on the point of breaking, I got up at 4 a.m. and began wandering aimlessly in the wooded hillside. This went on for some time until, unexpectedly, the words of the 130th psalm

30

sounded clearly in my mind: 'And plenteous redemption is ever found in Him; and, from all its iniquities, He Israel shall redeem.' With these words a light seemed to envelop me, and there flowed into my desolate heart such a flood of Love and Compassion that I was overwhelmed and overpowered by the weight of it. I was stricken by such wonder and amazement that I burst into tears of joy: it seemed to flow through my whole being with a cleansing and healing virtue. From that moment I knew that Love was the nature of reality. I was fit and well again. The experience is as real today as it was them . . ."

(3) F m 39: ". . . I was walking, *cold and disgruntled,* with the children. Then I became aware of an area of light to my right. I did not look. Why, I do not know. I looked at the children and they were not aware of what I sensed. Slowly, but definitely, I felt the tautness of my cold, contracted facial muscles smooth. It was a physical experience out of keeping with my normal reactions to the cold air around me. At this point, time seemed to stop. I was not aware of moving or anything except the unwrinkling of taut muscles and the waving light which I knew I was choosing not to look at. Inside I had a feeling of being very 'shy' and of an awareness that I was 'declining something' . . ."

That was all — comparatively little one might think, but it made such an impact on me. I looked at the children, they were still ambling along, those with me showed no awareness either of what I felt or that I had stopped — if indeed I had — or shown any signs of the extraordinary experience I had had. I looked to the right — but nothing, yet before I had not been prevented from doing so, but had not, as I had felt over-awed. I was cold again, but exhilirated. The holiday was a success and I enjoyed it and the children . . . The feeling of well-being and cheerfulness lasted a long time after I came back but it was many weeks before I self-consciously tried to describe my experience to a rather puzzled husband . . ."

(4) F m: ". . . I was exceedingly anxious and self-reproachful over this matter of improper feeding of the infant, which had been due to the fact that immediately after his birth I had experienced the strange phenomenon of falling in love

at first sight with a complete stranger who happened to be a visitor in my house . . . I lived an entirely domestic life in Naini Tal, but it was my habit after giving my small son his 6 a.m. bottle feed to dress quickly and having handed him to the nurse, climb up a steep zigzag path at the back of our chalet to a ridge which commanded a magnificent view of the Himalayas — Trisul, Nanda-Devi range. The climb was steep but short and at the top of the ridge was a long level path. It was my habit to walk along this path and sit down by a large boulder for a few moments gazing at the clear-cut panorama of the mountains against the ice-blue, early morning sky . . . In the last week in May that year, 1940, I climbed as usual one morning and sat down in the Buddha posture as was my habit by the boulder and gazed at the snows. Before doing so I glanced at my watch, because I had to be back in good time that day, as I was taking the little girls down to the Bazaars on a shopping expedition. My watch said it was 7.20 a.m. I then looked up at the snows — but immediately I lost all normal consciousness and became engulfed as it were in a great cloud of light and an ecstasy of knowing and understanding all the secrets of the Universe, and a sense of the utmost bliss in the absolute certainty of the perfection and piercing purity of goodness in the Being in whom it seemed all were finally enclosed, and yet in that enclosure utterly liberated. I 'saw' nothing in the physical sense . . . it was as if I were blinded by an internal light, and yet I was 'looking outward'. It was *not* a dream but utterly different, in that the 'content' was of the utmost significance to me and in Universal terms. Gradually this sense of ecstasy faded and slowly I came to my ordinary senses and perceived I was sitting as usual and the mountains were as usual in daily beauty. I glanced at my watch and found the minute hand had barely moved — my experience had taken a matter of seconds in earthly time, but I seemed to have moved in Eternity.

I went down the hill and had breakfast with my children and all day long the aftermath in the form of a wonderful mental and spiritual glow delighted me . . ." [32]

One contributor was threatened with bereavement —

(5)   F m: ". . . My father, who is now 84 years of age, was rushed

via ambulance to the hospital ten years ago. Four hours later, our doctor told us that my father would not live through the night. I went to the Chapel at St. Joseph's Hospital, which was on the first floor, and went up to the first row of seats and just sat. I was numb and shocked. As I stared towards the altar, a very soft light became brighter and larger. I immediately knelt and felt a warm glow engulf me. All that I said in a soft voice was: "God, please spare Papa so that we can have some happy times together." The glow left. I left the Chapel knowing my father would be all right. Sure enough, he lived . . ."

Three others had suffered bereavement. For one, the seeing of lights has been a daily occurrence ever since —

(6)   M w 80: ". . . Early in February 1964, strange lights began to appear in all parts of the room where I happened to be. Beautiful, pale blue, slowly fading in and staying for a few seconds, then slowly fading out. They were at their best in a darkened room while I was by myself and thinking of her. Sometimes they came singly, very bright and large, sometimes numerous and smaller. In about the middle of February, just before settling down for the night, the lights were extra numerous, 15 or 20 but more numerous than previously. While contemplating them and wondering as to their significance, a different light appeared — a golden flame colour, high up in the room, approximately 10 feet away. This startled me and brought an exclamation to my lips — unfortunately so — as the Flame Light immediately vanished and has never returned. The other lights are now a daily experience. Over the five years from my bereavement no day has passed but they appear . . ."

For another, the experience followed immediately on her husband's death —

(7)   F w: ". . . I had received an emergency call to my husband's bedside — he was dying of cancer. 'The end is near', the nurse said, and drew the curtains round the bed. I sat beside the bed in utter desolation — the worst moments I have ever known. There was a moving shadow as the breathing stopped, and then I lifted my eyes. Above the bed there was a shadow, but as I turned my head there was *a soft glow,* like

a light in fog, and moving 'ticker-tape' letters[2] forming into the three words TRUST IN GOD. Then it faded, the nurse came, and it was all over. I walked home from the hospital, and it was as if balm had been poured on a gaping wound . . . . ."

For the third, the experience occurred the same night —

(8) F 40: ". . . At the age of 15 I was evacuated to a village in Berkshire where I took a job in a private household. The mistress of the house had the task of telling me my brother had been killed in Italy. This was naturally a terrible shock. The same evening I went to bed as usual in a bungalow attached to the main building. It was a dark night and the employers had gone out to a party so the main house was in darkness. I mention this for a reason which will become clear later on.

Feeling utterly depressed and — as I am not 'religious' except for the usual Sunday School and occasional Matins (C of E) — also feeling *lost,* I pondered over the great mysteries — why are we born? Where are we going? What's life all about, etc. Suddenly there was *a misty ball of light* over towards the door of my room . . . My mind seemed to 'change gear'. I use car terminology to suggest a change of normal activity difficult if not impossible to describe. It was as if a voice spoke in my head 'Don't worry any more about X — he is quite well and happy'. On hearing this I suddenly felt quite relaxed after the great emotional storm of the day. I have never since then worried about the after-life and have been content to leave it in God's hands. During my years of agnosticism I have often recalled and tried to explain the foregoing experience to myself in terms of 'hysteria', 'overwrought imagination', etc. But today at age 40 I am convinced that it was real, true and not to be explained away, that it was a message to me in comfort and inspiration . . ." [15]

For some contributors the experience occurred while they were lying in bed (cf. (1) and (7) above) —

e.g. (9) M 57 (Dr.): ". . . I remember 43 years ago when aged 14, I was lying in bed in my home. It was about 10 o'clock I felt a sudden terrific happiness take hold of me. It was a unique

34

feeling of joy such as I had never felt before. And it dawned on me that there was one supremely simple and important thing — to love people, and to spread love. My eyes were fixed to the left hand corner of the ceiling and I saw *a red colour, rather like the glow of a fire,* and that seemed to love. I seemed to leave myself. After a few minutes I realised who I was and where I was. On reflection, what impressed me about this experience, apart from its quality of absoluteness and ultimate value, was that a Power had acted on me. I was inactive, receiving something and I did not exert my will. I was taken hold of. At no time have I ever doubted the absoluteness and ultimate value of this experience . . ." [14]

In one case, the bedroom light had just been switched off, and the experience occurred as an elaboration of the subject's after-image (cf. 1a (11)-(14) for visions based on the perception of actual objects) —

(10) F m: ". . . I was in bed, I had been looking at the light as I switched it off. This left me with a diminished circle of light in the blackness. But instead of diminishing to disappearance it reached a point at which it seemed to make a most moving and significant change and became, as it were, in control of itself and no longer subject to my visual mechanism. With a movement of its own it turned in upon itself like a rose folding its petals, and made what seemed an entirely voluntary act of disappearance. The strange thing was the feeling this conveyed of absolute love. It filled me with both awe and fear."

Several contributors' experiences occurred while walking, whether in company (cf. (3) above) or alone (cf. (2) above) —

e.g. (11) M 65: ". . . I was in Scotland and had been to the cubicle in my hut and *was walking back to the Mess* when suddenly a light shone on the wall of the passage with a cross clearly displayed, as though intense sunlight was coming through a window with the cross casting an intense shadow. There was in fact no window or source of light to account for what I saw.

The curious factor to me was that although in those days I was nervous of the dark and very impressionable, I had a curious feeling of comfort and a deep feeling of intense emotion. My brother was killed in France at about this time, but whether the events were coincidental or connected, I do not know . . ."

(12) M 33: ". . . About four or five times previously in my life I have felt that the Spirit of Christ (Truth) is very close to me, and has helped or guided me along life's way. The particular experience that I want to tell you about happened last Sunday week. I had been listening to a 11.30 service on the radio (I can't remember a thing about it now) and was *crossing our farmyard* preparatory to feeding some of the stock; I also remember that I was humming the first verse of 'There is a green hill far away', when suddenly I knew that I was in the presence of God. (For God could be substituted the Spirit of Truth, the Almighty, etc.) I managed to walk twenty yards to one of the sheds, where I bowed down[3] before One who was so much greater than I. I would not and could not open my eyes[4] at this time, but I know that with me in that shed was the living presence of Christ. I felt that there was a great Light in front of me[5], and till that instant I did not know what Humility meant; but out of the depth of my being came the realisation that I am not worthy that He should come to me. And as I knelt, the Light began to recede until it seemed to fade into the distant clouds, and when I opened my eyes the tears were streaming down my face, but they seemed to be tears of joy. The whole experience was so unexpected . . ."

For some the experience came in answer to prayer (cf. (4) above); for one, it was induced by meditation (cf. 1b (17) above) —

(13) F m 42: ". . . At one time, long before the Beatles, my curiosity and impulsiveness led me to try the Maharishi's idea — and I came to the result that there was something in it . . . The most unusual experience one of these meditation sessions gave me was that I felt as if I had been hit by a blinding light from a car headlight.[6] I had lost all sense of time, but could have sworn I hadn't been asleep. And you felt marvellously happy afterwards . . ."

One contributor's experience occurred (like C. S. Lewis'

conversion) while travelling in a bus (cf. 1b (14) above, and 1e (22) below) —

    (14) F m: ". . . The greatest gift I have ever been given and experienced was Everlasting Life. I was just given it while travelling on a bus, and it was a wonderful joy and came as a ray[7] from outside. I looked to see if other people had seen or understood anything, but all was normal and I just wondered how or why I had received such a marvellous relevation."

Sometimes the experience seems to be triggered off, or at least preceded, by the occurrence of certain words to the subject — cf. (2) ". . . unexpectedly, the words of the 130th psalm sounded clearly in my mind . . . 'And plenteous redemption is ever found in Him; and, from all its iniquities, He Israel shall redeem'. With those words a light seemed to envelop me. . ."

    (12) ". . . I was humming the first verse of 'There is a green hill far away', when suddenly . . ."

Sometimes the words constitute rather than precede the experience —

e.g. (7) ". . . letters forming into the three words TRUST IN GOD . . . "

    (8) ". . . It was as if a voice spoke in my head: 'Don't worry any more about X — he is quite well and happy' . . ."

For one contributor, the reading of poetry triggered off the experience —

    (15) F m 63: ". . . Entranced by Robert Bridges' anthology of poetry. Read poem after poem. Filled with sense of beauty. Suddenly a point of bright light appeared, distant, but intensely bright light appeared, distant, but intensely bright. 'It must be God' flashed into my mind . . .".

At this point I must draw attention to a particular kind of trigger. Certain contributors mention that immediately before their experience they were preoccupied with the question of helping somebody else —

e.g. (1) ". . . The experience came after a period of emotional and mental upheaval, *and an appeal for help from outside* . . ."

cf. 1a (8) above: "... For several weeks previous to the occurrence I been devoting a great deal of time to a neighbour of ours, trying to help her in her strained mental state. One morning, about 5.45 a.m. after one such session the previous night..."

1b (9) above: "... A nephew of mine was very difficult... I prayed for him constantly and one night while praying..."

1b (18) above: "... In the early part of the evening I had been visited by a friend who needed my advice and help... I felt that my powers of comprehension and sympathy had grown in order to meet the problem..."

Next, *description of the light or lights* —

(1) "... what I took to be a luminous star which gradually came nearer, and appeared as a soft, slightly blurred white light.. ..."

(3) "... an area of light to my right... waving light..."

(4) "... engulfed as it were in a great cloud of light... and it was as if I were blinded by an *internal* light..."

(5) "... a very soft light became brighter and larger..."

(6) "... strange lights... beautiful, pale blue, slowly fading in and staying for a few seconds, then slowly fading out..."

(7) "... a soft glow, like a light in a fog..."

(8) "... a misty ball of light..."

(9) "... at the left hand corner of the ceiling... a red colour, rather like the glow of a fire..."

(10) "... a diminishing circle of light... turned in upon itself like a rose folding in its petals[8]..."

(11) "... a light shone on the wall of the passage with a cross clearly displayed, as though intense sunlight was coming through a window with the cross casting an intense shadow.. ..."

(12) "... a great Light in front of me... began to recede until it seemed to fade into the distant clouds..."

(13) "... as if I had been hit by a blinding light from a car headlight..."

(14) ". . . came as a ray from outside . . ."

(15) ". . . a point of bright light . . . distant, but intensely bright . . ."

Next, the *affective tone* of the experience —

(1) ". . . I was seized with violent trembling, but had no fear. I knew that what I felt was great awe[9]. This was followed by a sense of overwhelming *love* coming to me, and going out from me, then of great compassion from this Outer Presence. After that I had a sense of overpowering peace and indescribable happiness . . . The sequence of the sensations described have remained very clear, i.e. Awe, Love, Compassion and Peace — in that order . . ."

(2) ". . . there flowed into my desolate heart such a flood of *Love* and compassion that I was overwhelmed . . . burst into tears of joy . . ."

(3) ". . . Slowly, but definitely, I felt the tautness of my cold, contracted facial muscles smooth . . . At this point time seemed to stop . . . I knew I was choosing not to look at (the light). Inside, I had a feeling of being very 'shy' and of an awareness that I was 'declining something' . . . I felt overawed. I was cold again, but exhilarated . . ."

(4) ". . . an ecstasy . . . a sense of the utmost bliss . . ."

(5) ". . . I immediately knelt and felt a warm glow engulf me . . ."

(7) ". . . it was as if balm had been poured on a gaping wound . . ."

(8) ". . . I suddenly felt quite relaxed after the emotional storm of the day . . ."

(9) ". . . I felt a sudden terrific happiness take hold of me. It was a unique feeling of joy such as I had never felt before . . . I saw a red[10] colour, rather like the glow of a fire, and *that seemed to be love*. I seemed to leave myself . . . I was inactive, receiving someone, and I did not exert my will. I was taken hold of . . ."

(10) ". . . The strange thing was *the feeling this conveyed of absolute love*. It filled me with both awe and fear[11] . . ."

(11) ". . . The curious factor to me was that although in those days I was nervous of the dark and very impressionable, I had a curious feeling of comfort and a deep feeling of intense emotion . . ."

(12) ". . . I bowed down . . . I would not and could not open my eyes at this time . . . (cf. 1a (8); and (3) above . . . I was choosing not to look . . . 'shy', etc.) . . . till that instant I did not know what Humility meant . . . when I opened my eyes the tears were streaming down my face, but they seemed to be tears of joy . . ."

(13) ". . . I had lost all sense of time . . . felt marvellously happy afterwards . . ."

(14) ". . . it was a wonderful joy . . ."

So it is not just the depressed or bereaved that receive comfort and joy from this experience; the effect is general.

Three exceptions stand out —

(16) M 65: ". . . before my very eyes I saw a sight that will remain in my mind for as long as I live. I was looking towards the heavens and before me appeared a great piece of light travelling diagonally across the sky. It seemed to be not much higher than a telephone pole. It was trapezoid in shape — being four feet square and twelve or fourteen feet long. It appeared to be a self-illuminating glass-like box. What a strange sight! How unexpected! This was my first psychic experience . . ."

(17) M m 66: ". . . I was conducting investigations at a place called Keta near the Togoland border and had to stay at a Rest House near the sea. Going early to bed I was awakened by the cries of birds, the barking of dogs, etc. and was amazed to see a large bright light ascend from the sea and sway in the sky within my vision, and after some time it moved straight over the Rest House, and by getting out of bed and looking upwards from the window I could see it immediately overhead. A similar occurrence was repeated the following night. Exactly one month later I was 180 miles away from these recorded events, and at my house in Accra. I was awakened by a shout from my servant that there was a 'big moon' over the house. Putting on a gown I stood

outside and saw this huge bright light over the house. Again it was repeated and left me mystified . . ."

(18) F s: ". . . About three years ago, as I lay in bed and was about to pass from waking to sleeping, I saw before my eyes an extremely brilliant ball of light — a very intense light in a black background. The room was dark and I think my eyes were open; I saw the light for between 5 and 10 seconds. It was not caused by any physical condition of myself — I have very good health, nor light from outside, it was far, far too intense. About 3 or 4 weeks later I had the same experience under just the same conditions but this time the ball of light was surrounded by an equally intense line of light round the circumference just a short distance from it . . ."

Note the attitude of these three contributors: the light is a phenomenon; they are observers, carefully describing it ("not much higher than a telephone pole . . . trapezoid in shape", "after some time it moved straight over the Rest House", "I saw the light for between 5 and 10 seconds. It was not caused by any physical condition of myself"). The tone is objective. There is no question of an affective relation between self and light. Emotions do not enter into it. Now with these contrast a fourth account, which starts similarly —

(19) M 75: ". . . I had the following experience during the first week in March 1910, while watching for a friend in a Perthshire village. I was 17 at the time and working for my entrance examination (medical) to St. Andrews University. I was also about to become a confirmed member of the Scottish Episcopal Church like the other members of my family. Although I had not taken religion seriously, I was not unduly perturbed. The afternoon was dry but rather overcast, and I was in the open a short distance from the village. Suddenly the sky ahead of me became flame-coloured, and this was followed by such a feeling of utter peace and benevolence as to be quite impossible to forget. I think I can say truthfully that it altered my whole outlook on life, an experience compared with which all other things appear cheap and second rate." [17]

Where does the fundamental difference lie? You may say

"Both kinds of people have the same experience — see some sort of light — but they *interpret* it differently, the religiously inclined in terms of love, etc." But this is to get things the wrong way round. In the affective experience, the subject's *own emotions* contribute fundamentally to what he sees. It is a different order of experience — the pre-objective. He does not observe, he responds: and his response colours what he seems to see.

Another distinction is that made in 1b (p. 27) between two kinds of affective experience — the impersonally ecstatic and the personal encounter with a "You". Now (4), with its engulfing cloud of light, ecstasy of knowing all the secrets of the Universe, and sense of the utmost bliss, is a good example of the former (cf. 1b (1)) and (2), and 1d and f passim); (13) and (14) are also impersonal. But the rest (apart from the dispassionate experiences (16) - (18)) involve an affective *relation* with the light — feelings of awe, or love, or humility, or whatever.

Cognitive States

(1) ". . . Certainty about what I must do suddenly came to me . . ."

(2) ". . . From that moment I *knew* that Love was the nature of reality . . ."

(4) ". . . an ecstasy of *knowing* and understanding all the secrets of the Universe, and . . . absolute certainty of the perception and piercing purity of goodness . . ."

(5) ". . . I left the Chapel *knowing* my father would be all right. Sure enough, he lived . . ."

(9) ". . . it *dawned on me* that there was one supremely simple and important thing — to love people, and to spread love . . ."

(12) ". . . when suddenly I *knew* that I was in the presence of God . . . . till that instant I did not know what Humility meant; but out of the depth of my being came the *revelation* . . ."

(14) ". . . a marvellous *revelation*."

Duration

Apart from (4), the only contributor who could specify this was (as one might expect) one of the "dispassionate observers" — (18) ". . . I saw the light for between 5 and 10 seconds . . ." — otherwise the nearest anybody got was —

(9) ". . . *After a few minutes* I realised who I was and where I was . . .".

This failure to specify is not surprising when one considers how often the experience is described as involving the loss of sense of time (and space) —

e.g. (3) ". . . Time seemed to stop . . ."
(13) ". . . I had lost all sense of time . . ."
(4) ". . . I lost all normal consciousness . . ."
(8) ". . . I seemed to leave myself . . ."

Estimates of duration can often only be based on "external" evidence (in the absence of the subject's own sense of time) — cf. 1a (8) above: ". . . it could not have lasted for more than 3 or 4 seconds. My iron had done no damage to the laundry on the board . . .". The same applies to (4) — just before the experience: ". . . I glanced at my watch because I had to be back in good time. . . . My watch said it was 7.20 a.m. . . .". And just after it: ". . . I glanced at my watch and found the minute hand had barely moved — my experience had taken a matter of seconds . . . moved in Eternity . . ."[12]

The suddenness of the experience is stressed by some — e.g. ". . . unexpectedly . . ." (2), ". . . Suddenly . . ." (8), ". . . immediately . . ." (4), ". . . suddenly . . ." (9), ". . . suddenly . . ." (11), ". . . when suddenly . . . and . . . the whole experience was so unexpected . . ." (12), ". . . Suddenly . . ." (15), ". . . Suddenly . . ." (19).

After-effects

(1) ". . . I awoke in the morning with a feeling of having been transformed, and in the days that followed, I had a very much clearer sense of my identity, saw people more clearly and things in a different way. Certainty about what I must do

43

... suddenly came to me ... The desire to pray ... grew daily and I have kept up the habit ever since ... I have never since doubted ... nor lost a sense of eternity ..."

(2) "... From that moment I knew that love was the nature of reality. I was fit and well again. The experience is as real today as it was then ..."

(3) "... The feeling of well-being and cheerfulness lasted a long time after I came back ..."

(4) "... all day long the aftermath in the form of a wonderful mental and spiritual glow delighted me ..."

(6) "... a perpetual reminder ..."

(7) "... I walked home from the hospital, and it was as if balm had been poured on a gaping wound ..."

(8) "... I have never since then worried about the after-life and have been content to leave it in God's hands ... today at age 40 I am convinced that it (the experience) was real, true and not to be explained away ..."

(9) "... At no time have I ever doubted the absoluteness and ultimate value of this experience ..."

(13) "... felt marvellously happy afterwards ..."

(19) "... such a feeling of utter peace and benevolence as to be quite impossible to forget ... it altered my whole outlook on life, an experience compared with which all other things appear cheap and second rate."

Note that the experiences of (8) and (19) occurred in their teens, and that for (7) "never since" meant throughout 25 years, while for (18) the most striking experience of his life happened 58 years previously.

Language

I: A favourite metaphor is the hydraulic: "... there *flowed* ... such a *flood* of Love ... that I was overwhelmed and overpowered by the *weight* of it ..." (2); "... became *engulfed* ..." (4); "... felt a warm flow *engulf* me ..." (5); "... it was as if

44

balm had been *poured on* a gaping wound . . ." (7). More than that, "engulfed" suggests a dissolving of the normal barriers between "self" and "other", "inside" and "outside". The *passivity* of the experience is stressed: ". . . I was inactive, receiving someone . . . I was taken hold of . . ." (9). A mechanical metaphor: ". . . My mind seemed to 'change gear' . . ." (8) — was justified by the *ineffability* of the experience — "I use car terminology to suggest a change of normal activity difficult if not impossible to describe." cf. (20) F m 78: ". . . *inexpressible* feelings as of a light within or around me at certain times . . ." and ". . . The nearest I could come to describing it was (to speak of) my consciousness 'going up into the sun'" (cf. (8) ". . . I seemed to leave myself . . .").

II: *Paradox*: e.g. (4) ". . . the Being in whom it seemed all were finally enclosed and yet in that enclosure utterly liberated . . . (cf. the Church of England prayer ". . . Whose service is perfect freedom . . ."); and ". . . I 'saw' nothing in the physical sense . . . it was as if I were blinded by an internal light, and yet I was 'looking outward' . . .".

III: *Qualification*. As one would expect, the three "dispassionate observers" used direct, unqualified terms: ". . . before me appeared a great piece of light" (16), ". . . was amazed to see a large bright light . . ." (17), ". . . I saw before my eyes an extremely brilliant ball of light . . ." (18). But a large number of other contributors (significantly larger than in 1b) also spoke without qualification — ". . . I became aware of an area of light . . ." (3), ". . . a very soft light became brighter and brighter . . ." (5). ". . . lights began to appear . . ." (6), ". . . there was a soft glow . . ." (7), ". . . there was a misty ball . . ." (8), ". . . I saw a red colour . . ." (9) (but he goes on, ". . . that *seemed* to be love. I *seemed* to leave myself . . ."), ". . . a light shone . . ." (11), ". . . a point of bright light appeared . . ." (15), ". . . the sky ahead of me became flame-coloured . . ." (19). With these, contrast the following: ". . . I *thought* I heard . . . but this *may have been imagined* . . ." (1), ". . . a light *seemed* to envelop me . . . , . . . it *seemed* to flow through my whole being . . ." (2), ". . . I became engulfed *as it*

45

were in a great cloud of light . . . it was *as if I* were blinded . . ." (4), ". . . it *seemed* to make a most moving and significant change . . ." (12) (but later he states directly ". . . the Light began to recede . . ."); ". . . *I felt as if* I had been hit by a blinding light from a car headlight". (13)

Chapter 1: c: Notes

1. Though I distinguish between descriptions of "light" (1b) and of "a light" (1c) they sometimes amount to much the same thing, as in 1b (15) and 1c (2, 4, 12 and 13).

2. cf. 1a (26) and (27).

3. cf. 1a (3), (8) and (9) on physical attitude.

4. cf. (3) above . . . "I did not look. I had a feeling of being very shy and . . . declining something . . ."

5. cf. 1b (18) ". . . The curious thing is that I *felt* the light."

6. cf. 1b (15) above: ". . . I was flooded with the most intense blue-white light . . . like looking into the face of the sun . . ."

7. cf.   Henry Vaughan:
   I saw Eternity the other night
   Like a great ring of pure and endless light.

8. cf. C. G. Jung on the "mandala".

9. The distinction is interesting. Contrast (9) ". . . filled me with both awe and fear".

10. cf. 1b (9): ". . . a warm orange-coloured glow".

11. We do not find the feeling of love conveyed by the light so strange, in view of other similar accounts. But what does seem strange in this case is the combination of love and fear.

12. This despite the fact that "*Gradually*, this sense of ecstasy faded and *slowly* I came to my ordinary sense . . ." before she looked at her watch.

1: d: A FEELING OF UNITY WITH ONE'S SURROUNDINGS[1]

(1)   F s: ". . . As I sat on a low wall opposite a beautiful tree covered with pink blossom, thrown into a relief by the high hill behind it, I was suddenly made aware of my surroundings in a manner difficult to describe in words.

     The tree became vibrant, 'real' (in the sense that the 'burning bush' did to Moses in the O.T.) and I was transported into what I can only term 'reality' and was filled with a great surge of joy (i.e. like C. S. Lewis's *Surprised by Joy*) — this was fundamental and I was 'caught up into it' and *was part of it*. I felt a great sense of awe and reverence, permeated by the presence of a power which was completely real and in which I had my part to play. I knew that all was well and that all things were working together for good . . .

     The experience came instantly — I can't say how long it lasted — it corroborated what I have known and experienced at other rare 'peak' moments during my life."

Note the following:
1. Change in appearance of surroundings: ". . . The tree became vibrant, 'real' . . ." (cf. 1b (11) above, 1f (b) below).
2. Change of mood: ". . . transported . . . filled with a great surge of Joy . . .".
3. Change in relation to surroundings: ". . . I was 'caught up into it' ('reality') and was *part of it* . . ."
4. Attitude: ". . . awe and reverence . . . a power in which *I had my part to play* . . ."
5. Cognitive state: "I *knew* that all was well and that all things were working together for good . . ."
6. Onset of experience: ". . . came instantly . . ." (i.e. suddenly).
7. Ineffability: ". . . in a manner difficult to describe in words . . ."

(2)   M 37: "The phenomenon invariably occurs out of doors, more often than not when I am alone, although it has occurred when I have been in company with others. It is generally prefaced by a general feeling of 'gladness to be alive'. I am never aware of how long this feeling persists but after a period I am conscious of an awakening of my senses.

Everything becomes suddenly more clearly defined; sights, sounds and smells take on a whole new meaning. I become aware of the goodness of everything. Then, as though a light were switched off, everything becomes still, and I actually feel as though I were part of the scene around me. I can identify with the trees or the rocks or the earth and, with this identification, and the tremendous stirring within me, it seems as though I am looking at the human race, and myself in particular, through the wrong end of a telescope. I feel as though I have the power to do anything, no problem is too great for me to tackle — and with this feeling comes an ineffable sense of peace and well being.

Just as suddenly as it began it ceases and I find myself back, as it were, in reality again with the exception that the feeling of peace and well-being remains with me and stays with me sometimes for many weeks. Unlike the experience which occurs in the presence of great music, and which often makes me feel close to tears, this latter experience I have described seems to have no emotional involvement whatever other than desire to be more tolerant which is perhaps another way of showing more love to others . . .

Although I am not a conventionally religious person I came to the conclusion that the 'stillness and identifying' stage of the experience would be what a mystic or member of the clergy might call 'the Presence of God'. Further, because I cannot bring myself to accept a God who is totally outside us as persons, I concluded that it was God within me who was making his Presence felt. This latter point has proved of tremendous comfort to me because, by means of my experience, I have a direct line of communication to God which no amount of praying or church-going would bring me."

Again we may note certain common characteristics:

1. It happens "out of doors", and "more often than not when I am alone".

2. First, there is "a feeling of 'gladness to be alive' ". Then "Everything becomes suddenly more clearly defined . . ." and "I become aware of the goodness of everything".

3. Next, "everything becomes still, and I . . . feel . . . *part of* the scene around me. I can *identify with* the trees, etc . . ."

4. "... *Power* to do anything, no problem ... too great for me".
5. "... sense of peace and well-being ..."
6. "... Just as suddenly as it began it ceases ...", but "the feeling of peace and well-being remains and stays with me sometimes for many weeks ..."

   (3)   M 74 (Dr., Greek): "Between the years 1909 and 1915 and again between 1930 and 1939, when I was living in the Island of Corfu, Greece, I had the following experience on a dozen occasions or more.

       Each time I was alone and confronted by a beautiful landscape, or (less often) by a brilliant starlit night. The first symptom was a sudden hush that seemed to envelop me — this was subjective, however, as my hearing and all my other senses appeared actually to be keener than normal. Then, almost at once, I had a strange feeling of expansion which I find very difficult to describe. It seemed that, in some way, I was extending into my surroundings and was becoming one with them. At the same time I felt a sense of lightness, exhilaration and power as if I was beginning to understand the true meaning of the whole Universe.

       Unfortunately, this state never lasted for very long (only a few minutes I think) as it was easily dispelled by any sudden sound — in one case, by a dog barking in the distance. But the sense of exhilaration would often persist for half an hour or more. I use the expression 'exhilaration' and not 'ecstasy' because I always remained completely aware of my surroundings and could have 'broken the spell' had I wanted to do so, just by moving.

       I have tried to observe if any 'laws' could be discerned, and have made the following tentative list.

1.   I was always alone.
2.   I was always in the presence of great natural beauty.
3.   The feeling came on suddenly and could never be induced.
4.   Heat appeared to help, i.e. warm summer weather, usually around noon.
5.   A pleasant monotonous sound helped. The singing of cicada, the wind through pine branches, the lisp of a quiet sea.
6.   A pleasant fragrance also helped, especially that of wild

thyme. In one case (night and stars) a nearby lemon orchard.

I have described this experience in the following lines which, perhaps, sum up the situation better than prose.

Sky and reflecting sea with stars were filled,
A lemon orchard in the nearby gloom
Exhaled its fragrance and a cricket trilled.
And every essence by the night distilled
— scent, starlight, sound — was woven on a loom
Of transmutation, twining me till I
Had blended into earth and sea and sky . . ."

Note the initial "sudden hush" (cf. (2) ". . . everything becomes still . . ."); then the description of the actual experience — "a strange feeling of *expansion* which I find very difficult to describe" (cf. (1) ". . . difficult to describe in words . . .") — "It seemed to me that, in some way, I was *extending into* my surroundings" (cf. (1) ". . . caught up into . . .") — "and was becoming *one with* them" (cf. (2) ". . . as though I were *part of* the scene around me . . ."); ". . . I felt a sense of . . . power . . ." (cf. (2) ". . . I feel as though I have the power to do anything . . ."); and then the cognitive aspect — ". . . as if I was beginning to *understand* the true meaning of the whole Universe . . ." (cf. (1) ". . . I *knew* that all was well . . . I had my part to play . . ."). The poem vividly expresses the feeling of unity — ". . . woven on a loom of transmutation, *twining* me till I had *blended* with . . ." — also the passivity of the experience.

(4) M 32: ". . . I began my National Service in the army in 1958 when I was 21. In March 1959 I was at home (in Exeter) on leave. I had arrived home with a high temperature and spent nearly a week in bed (I was at home for about a fortnight altogether). One afternoon I was lying in bed, nearly ready to get up, but still feeling rather weak. I had been glancing at some holiday brochures and was wide awake. It was a beautiful sunny day, and I began looking at the hills which I could see from my window. What followed is almost impossible to express in words, but my whole mode of perception and my whole being suddenly altered. For what I think was a brief instant, though it seemed to last for a long time, I seemed to be 'at one' with the hills, to be identified

with them, to belong to them. My whole being was absorbed in this feeling, which was of great intensity . . . Then the 'focus' altered, and I was looking at the hills normally again, but feeling very startled at what had happened. I puzzled over it for weeks. I have a great love of the countryside, and for hills, and sometimes have feelings of exaltation when walking among the hills, but no more, I think, than many other people have — certainly nothing special. The experience I have written about was totally different in kind to anything else I have known, and it has never been repeated . . ."

1. ". . . my whole *mode of perception* and my whole *being* suddenly altered . . ." — The double change (in appearance of/relation to surroundings) is characteristic, cf. (1) "The tree became vibrant"/"I was caught up into it and was part of it"; (2) "Everything becomes suddenly more clearly defined"/"I feel as though I were part of (it)";
(3) "My . . . senses appeared . . . keener than normal"/"It seemed to me . . . I was extending into my surroundings".
2. ". . . suddenly . . ." — The suddenness of the experience is stressed in all four accounts.
3. ". . . almost impossible to describe in words . . ." — The only contributor not to make this point is (3) who resorts to poetry.

(5)　M: ". . . I saw at my feet a small leaf, perhaps an inch long; pointed, withered to bright chestnut but still smooth. It was supported above the soil on the grey points of short grasses which did not bend beneath its weightlessness. It was curved in all three planes. Fibrous veins displayed its structure. It was quite still.

And as I watched, its stillness spread[2]; first to me. I wanted not to move by a hair's breadth, lest the bond between it and me should break. The stillness spread to the grass around us. It encompassed the hill. The beech wood became attendant on it. The whole valley slowly filled with it. This leaf and I, its participant, had drawn the miles-wide landscape into an attentive, breathless synthesis, focussed here, on this inch-long form, poised on its supporting grass points. And for some timeless space there was no movement, no sound and no distinction or identifying of parts in all that had been there united. For there was no "I" that gazed: No tiniest fraction of me stood aside to watch me watching. I and what I watched *were one*; and through that tiny gateway I became one with what was boundless.

Then this lostness slowly passed. I became aware of my feet in their heavy shoes, upholding my weight on their arched muscles; of the grey winter grass around me; above all, of the leaf, but now as a separate form, fugitive and transient, beautiful and still charged with a strange excitement, which was fading now as from some happening which was over and would not come again . . ."

So far I have pointed out resemblances between accounts. Now some differences —

Frequency: For (4) the experience "has never been repeated"; (1) however speaks of "other *rare* 'peak' moments"; for (3) the experience occurred "on a dozen occasions or more" while living in Corfu; but (2) differs from these (and all other accounts of the same type of experience) by saying "Although it is not a common experience I find *I can induce it*[3] after a certain amount of effort, the effect being so long-lasting that once or twice in a year is sufficient to carry me through all the sort of day-to-day problems that beset us."

Emotion: (1) was "filled with a great surge of joy", and so were most others; but for (2) the experience "seems to have no emotional involvement whatever" (perhaps there is a connection between this and the fact that he can induce it). One other contributor refers to his experience as "impersonal" —

(6) M 22: "On a number of occasions, I have experienced an extreme state of well-being which I considered, even at the time, to be of a different order of experience than e.g. happiness.

The feeling is very objective in that it is impersonal and, apparently, has little connection with my personal situation. I am filled with a warm glow that *connects me with the external universe with which I seem to become as one.* I transcend the trivia of everyday life and accept everything; good and evil, rich and poor, ugly and beautiful, without irritation. It is a sort of glorious indifference. Also these moods give a feeling of tremendous fertility, although I have never, to my knowledge, received any inspiration for creative activity for them. However, the feeling is similar to what I have felt when writing poetry, but far less active. It is an overwhelming potential which does not necessitate, indeed would be prohibited by, any specific action or thought. It is more the suspension of the senses or the complete coalition of them into a new and more complete sense. Even the pores of the body seem to be seeing, feeling, touching, smelling, hearing. More alive.

I have always been alone and close personal contact destroys. Personality is clearly inconsistent and the feeling is irresponsible in its indifference.

Generally the weather is warm and I am wandering through my home town Bath. I have felt the same elsewhere and in rain, but only once or twice . . .

I don't think I have ever felt this in unpleasant or uncomfortable conditions, but only in Bath, Edinburgh and in the country . . ."

For some the emotions were not altogether pleasurable —

e.g. (7) F 63: ". . . connected also with grief and loss . . . a vast overwhelming longing . . ."[4]

(8) F 57: "I was walking along a road in my home town (Eastbourne) approaching an incline where the road branched and straight ahead was an old flint wall covered with ivy. I had the feeling of everything opening out (or a veil being lifted) and a wonderful feeling of freedom (lightness) and of comprehension of everything. It's so hard to describe. I remember feeling exquisitely happy and saying to myself, 'So that is what it is all about'. I cannot say what I saw — it was like infinity and a radiance at the same time. Very, very brief and I was amazed to find myself still walking along the road, still about 200 yards from the ivy. . . . I had only a feeling of being bereft and sad . . ."

(9) F: ". . . a feeling of desolation, a sort of pure sadness . . . marvellous, uplifting . . . but with an element of pain."

(10) F 60: ". . . a feeling of unspeakable joy coupled with a desire for a form of fulfilment — as though there was a meaning — a wholeness to which one could belong if one but knew how.

When twelve years old I was on a beach. It was early

evening, the sun going down, the tide receding leaving little pools and runnels of water and firm wet sand. The sense of light and space was overwhelming. I felt frustrated (for want of a better word) in not belonging wholly to what was around me.

The same feeling occurred when I was thirteen, sitting on a hillside in the mid-day sun and overlooking a spreading green countryside.

The next occasion came in my thirties when bathing one sunny morning in a rough sea on a wide empty beach. I could have shouted from sheer exhilaration but again experienced this yearning for completeness and the feeling of something beyond what my senses told me . . ."[5]

(11) F 55: ". . . the feeling was as if I suddenly, that very moment, became aware of the answer to the mystery of life and the knowledge of it made me want to shout with joy, it seemed at that moment so simple. I wondered why everyone didn't see it and feel it and be bursting with joy!

. . . always this same feeling, leaving me weeping with a great joy and feeling of deep reverance and feeling of worship and love. I think it is best described as a sort of 'home-sickness', a 'nostalgia for some other-where' . . ."

(N.B. (7) - (11) are all female).

Cognitive States

As regards grasping the secret of the universe, some like (11) evidently felt they had got there, but a few others, like (10) felt they had stopped just short:

(12) F: ". . . a feeling that the wonderful answer to all things is just and only just beyond our grasp."

(13) F 60: "From the time I was a child I had occasionally what I now realise was a mystical experience. I particularly remember an occasion in my teens when I looked out of a window at a tree and knew that the tree and I were one. But instead of losing myself in the oneness (which is the usual mystical experience, isn't it?) I seemed to be reaching an apprehension of what this signified. I felt myself 'going somewhere' and drew back in fear because I thought that I

55

should not 'get back' again."

(14) F 43: ". . . At both times — once about five years ago — and the last about two years ago — I was outdoors, the first time working on my garden, towards noon-time — to the best of my knowledge engrossed in planting and weeding — when I 'felt' a presence or the feeling of someone or something. I looked up and around but was apparently alone. The feeling persisted but I was not frightened, and I do remember thinking that the day was uncommonly quiet[6]. I continued planting, but something caused me to want to stand and just sort of look at the beauty of the day and enjoy the moment more fully. I stood, and then I had a rush of warmth and tremendous well-being and felt — for a fleeting second — an overwhelming unity with the sky and earth and all of nature; and then I felt a fear and made myself 'let go' — but I had the strange sensation that if I had "held on' I would have been aware of secrets and information beyond human knowledge.

The second event, about three years later, again came 'out of the blue'. I had brought my sons to summer camp and was driving home — about 5.30 p.m. one summer evening — actually I was hurrying to meet my husband for dinner and the theatre. The road from their camp winds down a mountain — at one point has a fantastic view of the valley at the foothills. I was driving onward — and when I came to the view spot, the sun was hitting the village below in such a way, it appeared a rosy bronze. Although I was hurrying I decided to stop a moment and fully admire the scene. I remember thinking 'I wish I could paint; these are the scenes I would put on canvas.' I got out of the car, and the experience was similar to the previous (one) but far more intense in the feeling of a presence nearby. I felt if I held my breath I would hear breathing — and again I had the sense of well-being; but this time I knew — I don't know how — that if I 'held on' I would have information revealed to me, and I felt 'not worthy' or 'not ready' for such a revelation — but it took physical effort to 'come back' . . ."[7]

This was a feeling of exalted joy — I recall, only now, actually smiling, radiant like, both times, before the feeling of fear or unworthiness came upon me . . ."

56

(15) F 40: "When I was about 11 years old I spent part of a summer holiday with an aunt in the Wye Valley. Waking very early one bright morning, before any of the household was about, I left my bed and went to kneel on the window-seat, to look out over the curve which the river took just below the house. The trees between the house and the river — I was on a level with their topmost branches — were either poplars or silver birch, and green fields stretched away beyond the river to the far distance. The morning sunlight shimmered on the leaves of the trees and on the rippling surface of the river. The scene was very beautiful, and quite suddenly I felt myself on the verge of a great revelation. It was as if I had stumbled unwittingly on a place where I was not expected, and was about to be initiated into some wonderful mystery, something of indescribable significance.

Then, just as suddenly, the feeling faded. But for the brief seconds while it lasted I had known that, in some strange way I, the essential 'me', was a part of the trees, of the sunshine, and the river, that we all belonged to some great unity. I was filled with exhilaration, an exultation of spirit.

This is one of the most memorable experiences of my life, of a quite different quality and greater intensity than the sudden lift of the spirit one may often feel when confronted with beauty in Nature."

The next account is interesting in that the experience occurs simultaneously with the attainment of an eagerly sought goal. Also, the writer (paradoxically) feels more than usually aware of his own identity at the very moment of its diffusion.

(16) M 25: ". . . Earlier in the week, I had caught a glimpse of a buzzard flying over a loch, and being particularly interested in birds of prey (my interest is more aesthetic than anything else) I hoped to see some more . . . Although it is unreasonable I felt as though something was compelling me to go on looking, but by four o'clock I was sick of the hills, the heather, the sun and everything under it. I decided to return to my camp site and start packing for my return home the next morning . . . I can't express how dejected I felt as I walked (limped) back. Everything seemed pointless

including myself. I seemed to be lost in a whirlpool of thoughts that went round and round; all questions and no answers[8]. I was completely oblivious of my surroundings and walking automatically as if in a trance. Then I heard a sound behind me that I had never heard before and when I turned round to investigate I saw four buzzards directly overhead. I felt as if they had called to let me know they were there. From the moment I turned I felt all the fatigue drop away, all the pessimism and anxieties. The feeling of being narrow and cut off from something became a feeling of being vast and unbounded as if I was connected with the whole universe. I understood William Blake's poem 'To see a world in a grain of sand', everything including the stones on the path seemed to be infinitely significant. As I watched the buzzards spiralling in the blue sky I felt identified with them and yet at the same time I was intensely aware of my own identity; I felt as though I were the centre of the universe and at the same time the centre was everywhere . . ." [19]

Duration

Many contributors lost all sense of the passage of time during the experience: e.g. (1) ". . . I can't say how long it lasted . . ."; (4) "For what I think was a brief instant, though it seemed to last for a long time . . ."; (5) ". . . for some timeless space . . ." — cf. T. S. Eliot's "moments out of time." This point was enlarged upon by Mrs. Mary Wilson, the former Prime Minister's wife, in an account she recently gave on television:

"I was alone on a beach on the Island of Tresco, early one morning in summer. There was no-one else there, no houses in sight, and no boats passing.

I suddenly felt, in a way, disembodied — that the sea and the sky and the sand were all part of me as I was part of them, and at the same moment I felt that Time as we know it — a road on which we travel from the past, through the present to the future, did not exist, but that past, present and future were one so that thousands of years in the future were the same, and that the whole 'Time' problem was solved at last.

I had a sensation of extraordinary happiness.

Then everything swung back into place, in the present once more."

More than fifty people wrote of experiencing feelings of oneness with their surroundings — a striking number to have reported an experience not specifically asked for.

Language

I shall next consider some of the different ways in which they describe the feeling. Favourite terms were: "a feeling of being at one with"; "a deep animal feeling of being 'part of it all' " (this was the least mystical description); "a 'something more than' feeling"[9]; "at one"; "caught up in another dimension"; "a joining up with"; "became one with"; "felt the oneness of everything"; "a strange 'shift' "; "a feeling of at-onement with"; "I felt part of"; "I seemed to be drawn right out of myself . . . I knew I was 'at home' . . . that this was reality . . ."; "as if I had slipped into another entirely new dimension of existence . . . Time stood still . . . I was *absorbed* in the universe . . ."; "identified with"; "extending into . . . becoming one with"; "in some strange way I, the essential 'me' was a part of . . ."; "feeling of the link and unity with . . ."; "alienation resolved into 'at-onement', 'homecoming' "; "a state of 'oneness' with . . . a feeling of union and relationship . . . an experience of expansion and a feeling of suffusion from within me — an expanding of 'oneness' "; "inter-relation feeling"; "seemed to absorb like a sponge the whole of nature — it and I becoming one"; "feeling at one with"; "part of"; "completely at one with the universe, an empty vessel free to be filled";[10] "feeling of loss of individuality"; "I felt my own personality dissolve and link up with the world around me"; "my feet became as roots in the earth turning on its axis"; "I was above the world and looking further than my own horizons . . . Also simultaneously I could feel the earth under me and right down to the centre of the earth. And I belonged to it and it belonged to me"[11]; "a feeling of being vast and unbounded as if I was connected with the whole universe"; "I felt as though I were the centre of the universe and

59

at the same time the centre was everywhere."

Next, what was it that they felt "at one" with? — "Reality"; "the scene around me"; "the trees or the rocks or the earth"; "a leaf"; "my surroundings"; "the hills"; "olive trees"; "swifts"; "the external universe"; "what was around me"; "a tree"; "the sky and earth and all of nature"; "the trees, . . . the sunshine, and the river"; "all things"; "all other living things"; "an all-well-ness beneficent in its essence"; "certain created (not man-made) things"; "the universe"; "the earth"; "the insects"; "all that was alive"; "the natural world"; "the world around me"; "the time/space state, the universe"; "the whole"; "the world"; "all things"; "the whole universe"; "some essence of the universal process"; "Man, Earth and Spirit"; "the heart of Nature"; "the universe"; "the Whole Universe"; "the natural world or Universe"; "the whole of nature"; "nature"; "the lark's song and the earth and sky"; "creation"; "four buzzards spiralling in the blue sky."

Some contributors described feelings of unity with people rather than things:

> (17) F 56: "About 1962 I spent four hours standing at a busy road centre in Birmingham (a city I hardly knew) with five or six others in a Peace Vigil. At the three previous Vigils in which I had taken part, I had felt cut off from — perhaps a little superior to — the general public hurrying past, and had spent much of my time trying to pray for them, for those at war and for world peace. On this occasion I found instead that I was overtaken by an intense feeling of affection for and unity with everyone round as they ran to catch buses, took children shopping or joyfully met their friends. The feeling was so strong that I wanted to leave my silent vigil and join them in their urgent living.[12]
>
> This sense of 'oneness' is basic to what I understand of religion. Hitherto I think I had only experienced it so irresistibly towards a few individuals, sometimes towards my children or when in love.
>
> The effect of the experience, has been, I think, a permanent increase in my awareness that we are 'members one of another' — a consequent greater openness towards all and a

widening of my concern for others . . ." [48]

(18) F 36: ". . . I should like to describe what happened after the birth of my second child. I was in a public ward and some time on the third day after his birth, a marvellous feeling of being joined with all other living things came to me, as if the 'I' part of myself faded away and became one with every other person. I felt comfortably in peace, at once divorced from reality and yet at one with it. This feeling only lasted a few minutes, but the memory of it is very clear . . . This experience had the effect of making me more acutely aware of other people's feelings, so that it was almost painful to talk to others for a while, so strong was this sense of being a part of them . . ."

— or with both —

e.g. (19) F 22: "I guess the best way to start is to tell you what LSD does to me and to those I know have taken it. Then you can understand more of what it means. At first one starts to smile, then ₊to feel slightly dizzy, to feel floating, to hallucinate. One's eyes get larger, the pupil dilates and everything is seen in triplicate. Then real hallucinations like amoeba under microscopes. Everything is seen through a wavy film in which float before your eyes beautiful patterns, great splotches of colour, always transparent, always moving. Sound echoes, comes in waves and 'knocks' one over. Birds singing in the morning is amazing. An 'acid head' (one who trips a great deal) will appreciate softer more complicated pop sounds, not the usual bang, bang, bang of the horrid discotheque. Colours will intensify, light becomes the total answer. And throughout it all one feels amazingly pure . . . There is a realisation that one is part of . . rocks, stones, water, fire and earth. One is an electric throb in the air. One is part of a star. Looking at oneself in the mirror one will see pores, veins and wrinkles 'breathing', moving and the effect is quite horrifying at first. Then one realises that this is what one is and suddenly one loves it. Look at your hands, they are full of moving blood and veins and hairs, it is exciting and the body seems very frail and one is thankful for it. One is very happy. Life is intensified . . .

The incredible definition of everything, the intensification of environment, the beauty of light and the knowledge that everyone on earth is made of tissues of stars, blood of the oceans, eyes of air and with little hearts pumping and trying so hard, all this makes life very bearable. I am not related to other men unless I am first related to earth, rocks and leaf, to grass, fish, cats and cattle. Then knowing what I am made of, I know the man next to me is made of me and we are as tangled physically as if our actual arteries came out of our skin and locked together so that we shared our blood. Rather horrifying but very safe."

For some the inanimate "became" animate as part of the experience: — cf. (19) "... pores, veins and wrinkles 'breathing'."

e.g. (20) F: "... My experience was of a typical mystical kind, yet I think stronger and more lasting than is usually reported. All of a sudden, when I was walking in the country near my home (not taking a walk, just going to the mail-box) everything came alive around me, and seemed to glow and *breathe* with animation — even the sticks and stones at my feet, and the mountain across the valley; the trees particularly I remember. It was a very beautiful and profoundly disturbing and frightening experience.[1] I know now that this is the kind of vision people have after taking mescalin. The effect did not fade for a long time; at night the stars came alive, and for a week or two, day and night, I saw things in this way. I did not tell anyone about it, and gradually the effect faded, though for many weeks I could reproduce it at will. I was filled at the same time with a *feeling of one-ness* with the world and of the unity of all things ...

... I had been under very great emotional strain for some years before the event, and this had become extreme in the immediately preceding months. I believe I had been forced back and back into myself until I reached the very depths of my nature and could go no further; when this happened I think there was an equally extreme reaction; I think the vision I had was a projection of what was within myself ...

It is a long time since this happened to me, nearly twenty years. I have never lost the general effect of the experience."

(cf. 1a (11) — (20) above, and 2d (1) below).

Chapter 1: d: Notes

1. We have already met examples of this associated with other "sensory" phenomena (cf. 1b (15) and 1b above). Now I consider it *per se*.

2. cf. (2) ". . . everything becomes still . . ."

3. Usually the passivity of the experience is stressed, and the person's inability to recapture it. *Drugs*, however, perhaps may induce it (see (19) below). A feeling of unity *with God* may result from *prayer* (see 7a below); but for the person this is "a gift of grace", not something deliberately induced. Feelings of unity transcending self, space and time — but also usually described as transcending, rather than merging with one's surroundings — may come from *meditation* (cf. 1b (17) and 1c (13)); but here again the person would hardly talk of "effort" to "induce" it; it happens — cf. Chuang-Tze:

   "You cannot take hold of it,
   But you cannot lose it.
   In not being able to get it, you get it,
   When you are silent, it speaks
   When you speak, it is silent."

   — masterly use of paradox.

   Also Lao-Tze:

   "The secret waits for the insight
   Of eyes unclouded by longing;
   Those who are bound by desire
   See only the outward shell."

4. cf. Wordsworth's "aching joys" *(Tintern Abbey, 1.84).*

5. cf. Richard Jefferies: ". . . After the sensuous enjoyment always came the thought, the desire: that I might *be* like this; that I might have the inner meaning of the sun, the light, the earth, the trees and grass translated into some growth of excellence in myself . . ." (*The Story of My Heart*, Chapter 5).

6. cf. (2) "everything was still", and (3) ". . . a sudden hush".

7. The same difficulty occurs in some "out-of-the-body" experiences — see 1e (9), (14) and (17), and cf. (13) above: "I thought I should not 'get back' again."

8. Contrast 1b (2) above: ". . . I was my own questioner and answerer, and fast as the questions came, out trundled the answer, so easy to comprehend and always, always right . . ."

9. cf. Wordsworth "A sense sublime of something far more deeply interfused . . ."

10. cf. Keats (letter to R. Woodhouse): "A poet . . . has no identity — he is continually informing and filling some other body . . ."

11. cf. Richard Jefferies (*The Story of My Heart*, p.28) "I now became lost and absorbed into the being or existence of the universe. I felt down deep into the earth under, and high above into the sky, and farther still to the sun and stars. Still farther beyond the stars into the hollow of space, and losing thus my separateness of being came to seem like a part of the whole."

12. Contrast e.g. (6): "I have always been alone and close personal contact destroys." But is it such a contrast? A silent vigil may be a form of solitude, even in the middle of busy Birmingham.

13. cf. (13) and (14) who both mention fear. Also Laing: "James told of how, when walking on a summer evening in the park alone, watching the couples making love, he suddenly began to feel a tremendous oneness with the whole world, with the sky and trees and flowers and grass — with the lovers too. He ran home in panic and immersed himself in his books. He told himself he had no right to this experience, but more than that, he was terrified at the loss of identity involved in this merging and fusion of his self with the whole world." (*The Divided Self,* p.91).

14. cf. (2) "I find I can induce it after a certain amount of effort."

I: e. "OUT OF THE BODY" EXPERIENCES

Most religions distinguish between one's body and "soul" (or self). The body tends to be down-graded by comparison with the soul — Plato describes it as the prison of the soul. Among early Christians, Plotinus "seemed ashamed to be in the body" (Porphyry) and called it the soul's tomb ("soma sema"). The physical circumstances of birth were also felt to be degrading ("Inter faecem et urinam nascimur" — St. Augustine), not to mention the lusts of the flesh. For the Gnostics (as for Plato) the immortal soul parted company with the body at death; for orthodox Christians resurrection included the body — but it was nothing to be proud of ("If thine eye offend thee, pluck it out", etc.); St. Paul was particularly down on it ("the flesh" tends to be mentioned in the same breath as "the Devil"; contrast Solomon's attitude in the Old Testament "Song of Songs"). Nowadays the doctrine of the separate existence of body and soul — known as "dualism" and blamed chiefly on the French philosopher Descartes — gets short shrift from behaviourist critics, who refer to it as "the dogma of the ghost in the machine".

But "dualism" is not just the invention of a philosopher; it stands for something widely felt in human experience, and by people unacquainted with philosophy.

e.g. (1)   F s 50: "As a small child the earliest memory I have is a distinct feeling that "I" and my body were quite separate things, and I always felt I could get outside my body if I wished to. As an adult this once happened to me."

This feeling of "separateness" seems to be most commonly experienced when the subject is relaxed and passive —

e.g. (2)   M 27: "Whenever I lie motionless in bed I feel I have two identities — the physical one and the non-physical one. It is a strange but neutral experience."

I shall go on to describe cases where the person feels as if he has left his body and is seeing his surroundings (often including his own body) from a quite different point of view, (which is why I class this as a "visual" experience). But first we may consider some examples connected with worship —

(3)   M 68: ". . . Once while out in a field on a well-travelled

pathway, across a neighbouring farm of low rolling hills, I was thinking deeply on the subject of Jesus as the Son of God, and some of the miracles recorded in the Bible.

I lifted my eyes heavenward and seemed to see Jesus there in the clouds before me; I began running towards him as fast as I could run — there came into my mind this question: Is this the hour — am I to go now? As long as I kept my eyes and my mind on him I kept rising, running very fast, but not tiring at all. When I realised that I was several feet above the ground and had passed over a wagon gate across the path or roadway, I became afraid I might fall. The clouds covered him from my view. I looked earthward and was soon back down running, on the ground. No longer was He visible in the clouds, and I was once again an earthbound creature as before."

Here there is no question of leaving the body: our contributor rises, body and all, "several feet above the ground"[1] running all the while. This is in response to a vision; and he asks himself "Am I about to die?" — a common thought in the circumstances, as we shall see.

(4) F m 50: ". . . I felt he (my dying husband) might be aware of my presence although unconscious, and took his hand and closed my eyes. Immediately my surroundings disappeared from my conscious mind and I was aware of two distinct things happening at once — the reverence for the presence of God on my left hand side, powerful in its effect, and then I was swiftly being propelled into a vast current into space that is almost indescribable . . ."

Here the contributor experiences not a vision, but a sense of presence (both commonly occur to the bereaved); she does not run but is "swiftly propelled", and not over familiar ground but with eyes shut "into space"; whether she retains her body or not is not specified, but at any rate the experience is a passive, rather than a physically active one as in (3).

(5) F m 51: ". . . On 6th December, 1964, (when I was 45) I sat in church in the evening after I had been to the communion rail. The Minister had irritated me in the way he pronounced particular words. I said something like "O God

(or Lord Jesus, I am not sure which), make this more real to me" . . . then, suddenly, I was filled from within and that was real because it had never happened before. It was as if it filled me like a balloon is filled, nearly as if I was lifted. I am speaking of the upper half of my body and arms. Tears began to drop. It was all very brief . . ."

A prayer to God is followed by a feeling of "being filled"[2] "nearly as if I was being lifted". It is not the whole body that is affected, nor the unembodied soul, but "the upper half of my body and arms".

(6) M: ". . . While I was kneeling, praying as I had been taught to, praying but not feeling any special reality in prayer, I was touched and for a moment picked up — not that my body left the ground, but I had the clearest sensation of the part of me that is not the body being lifted up, and I remember thinking "What is happening to me?" The sensation was as clear as if it was physical. After a moment it passed and I was left wondering. I have since from time to time felt bent down with worship when praying, or in other ways deeply moved by worship, but these are emotional experiences and quite distinct from this first physical experience which has never recurred . . ."

This time it is not the body, not a part of it, but "the part of me that is *not* the body", which feels "lifted up". The expression is not used metaphorically, for "the sensation was as clear as if it was physical" and it is contrasted with mere "emotional experiences".

(7) M 79: ". . . The heavenly vision" was of Christ in overpowering glory. It was accompanied by the sensation of *leaving the body* . . . the better to worship . . ."

This connection between worship and "out of the body" experience is stressed by our next contributor, one of a small group of Christian women who meet together for prayer and, she says, share the experience —

(8) F m 55: ". . . We know also sometimes what it means to be 'outside our bodies' and able to look down from various distances away. On one occasion I was transported into space and saw the world far below and eventually was taken

up into the heavenlies . . ."

Now we turn to "out-of-the-body" experiences unconnected with worship (though sent in as "religious" experiences by those who had them). Most of these occurred while the person was lying in bed —

e.g. (9)　F m 46: ". . . In 1948 I had an out-of-the-body experience spontaneously, in broad daylight, for no obvious reason and being in perfect health. (At the time I did not know that such experiences are fairly frequent and well-documented). The experience itself was unsensational — for a while I contemplated my body which was lying on a divan, from underneath the ceiling; I felt splendidly liberated, light, and only a little surprised, and it became amply clear that the "I" was not in the body on the divan, but the consciousness which contemplated it. "I" returned into my body with the greatest reluctance — I knew I had to return — and since then I have been quite unable to fear physical death."

The experience was a pleasant one — "I felt splendidly liberated" — and, though associated with death, it removed all fear of death.

(10)　F m 44: ". . . I went to bed and had Astral Projection; I could see myself lying on the bed, and could also see my husband beside me. I was just above the bed, was out probably about 15-20 minutes (just guessing), and have never gone astral since . . ."

(11)　M m 29: ". . . I was in bed, my wife next to me, I must have been puzzling on death. *I seemed to be above where I lay . . . . . ."

— again the association with death.

(12)　M 73: ". . . The last unusual experience I had was about four years ago. I was in bed and I remember wondering if I was asleep or awake, as something seemed to be happening to me. I do not think I was dreaming, because everything was different. I had full control of my mind. Suddenly I seemed to be going at tremendous speed through space, but somehow my body was not with me. I could feel the vibrations of speed for a long time. I considered the fact that possibly I was having a dream, but I knew my mind was too

68

clear . . ."

Here, instead of hovering above the bed, looking down on his body, the disembodied person "seemed to be going at a tremendous speed through space" (cf. (4) above). It may have been a "lucid dream". Lastly, we may look back to 1a (23) who, describing a vision she experienced of her dog, says "*I seemed to slide out of myself* and stand by the bed".

None of the above say they were suffering from any illness at the time (and (9) emphasises that she was "in perfect health"). But a number of contributors had "out-of-the-body" experiences while *ill* in bed —

e.g. (13) F s 21: ". . . At the age of twelve when I was quite ill in bed, I found myself floating up from my body into a ray of sunshine. At the time I thought quite consciously that I was dying, and I remember that the feeling of liberation was joyful beyond anything else I have ever known. I didn't die, of course, but returned quite gently to my body. From that time on I've never been afraid of death . . ."

— Note the resemblance to (9): — "feeling of liberation"/"I felt splendidly liberated"; "From that time on I've never been afraid of death"/"since then I've been quite unable to fear physical death".

(14) F s 61: ". . . At 17 I had an experience of nearly dying, when very ill at boarding-school. I came out of my body and found myself lying about six feet above it, watching Matron and a doctor caring for me below. Something told me to fix this experience in memory, as it was very important and I had no difficulty in doing so as it was one of intense livingness, expansion, of well-being, with a tremendous magnetic pull to go on, out and away. I thought "If this is death, how lovely, natural, easy". Coming back was the reverse — very unpleasant, being cramped down into a painful, ill physical body. (My parents were sent for, and were told I had nearly gone in that night.) Since then I have never been afraid of death."

Again the pleasant feeling of liberation, this time described as "expansion", and the consequent loss of all fear of death.

(15) F m 71: ". . . Before the boy was born I had a burst ovary and

an internal haemorrhage from which I nearly died, and while in the British Hospital in Paris I floated to the roof at nights, and prayed God would not let me go up there ...".

Again the association with death, but this time the prospect was not welcomed ("prayed God not to let me go up there"); contrast (9) "I returned into my body with the greatest reluctance".

(16) F m 76: "... Once when all my family and myself were down with 'flu and I was delirious, I seemed to float on the air, and saw myself and my children lying in their beds ...".

(17) M m 66: "... One night I suddenly had a feeling of approaching death and said to my servant, "I shall never see my children again, for I am going to die". Shortly afterwards there was a flash of light, and I was "out of my body" looking down at my inert body on the bed. Almost immediately I passed through the bedroom wall, and had a sense of passing through a very deep blue or black atmosphere until I arrived at a place of tremendous light. I could see a lighted corridor and at the end of it was a "Being" shrouded in great light but it seemed that I received some kind of message to the effect that I had to "go back". Again I found myself speeding through the darkness and re-entering my bedroom where I saw my own body lying supinely on the bed apparently lifeless. The strange sensation of "re-joining" my cold, wet body gave me an extraordinary feeling, and I was conscious of great pain and weariness. In the morning I was taken by ambulance to the Ridge Hospital in Accra, and various tests were made, but although my blood had obviously been ravaged by some unknown virus, this was never isolated and within three weeks I had slowly recovered my health and resumed my duties."

The same contributor describes another "out-of-the-body" experience, in different circumstances:—

"... I was due to go on leave to the U.K. and through a series of strange events was initiated into Subud by an "opening" of the inner conscious. During this ceremony I experienced great joy and once again "passed out" of my body ..."

(18) F m: "... When 10 years old and recovering from mumps, I

floated to the ceiling and then part way round the room, when, realising what had happened, I decided that I had got very near the gaslight which was lit and that it was dangerous, so I floated back to the bed, looked down and found myself back in bed."

At first sight this looks very similar to (13) and others, but is it in fact an "out-of-the-body" experience? She nowhere speaks of leaving or rejoining her body ("I floated to the ceiling... floated back to bed") but her last sentence ("... *looked down* and found myself back in bed") suggests autoscopy after the event.

Next we may consider three cases of "out-of-the-body" experiences during (apparent) loss of consciousness —

> (19) M m: "... Yesterday evening I returned home as usual for a late tea which I shared with my wife and son, when I lost consciousness of all around me and my wife laid me on the sofa and took off my collar as they thought I had fainted. I found myself carried by the Angels on a marvellous journey. I could look back for a moment and see my own body lying on the sofa and my wife and son bending over me — then the sight of home vanished. I had come to the glorious golden gates of Paradise. A light more wonderful than the light of the sun, pervaded everywhere . . . Christ came up to me laying His hand upon me. "Well done, good and faithful servant, I have a little more work for you to do for me and then I will come and call you". The vision vanished, once more I returned to my body and in a short time was my usual self. But I knew it was no vain dream, no imagination. I really died, I really saw what Christ has prepared for them that love him."

The resemblance to (17) is striking — a feeling of death, a journey to a "place of tremendous light", "light more wonderful than the light of the sun", a meeting with a divine "Being", being told to "go back" — though for (19) the encounter was perhaps more reassuring ("Christ came up to me laying His hand upon me 'Well done, good and faithful servant' . . ." cf. 1a, p. 3 above, on affective relations in visions).

> (20) M s 30: ". . . One Saturday evening at 7 p.m. I had just finished tea, lit a cigarette and went into the kitchen to wash; when I got in, a lady from next door — was talking to my

mother. She had just buried her young son who had been burned to death. When hearing her describing the boy's suffering, I felt something in my stomach turn. I then went over to wash as I was going out for a drink. I had just turned round to get a towel when I felt a buzzing at the bottom of my spine. Then the feeling just went out of the bottom part of my body. I could not believe what had happened and just stood startled. I stood for about two minutes, when suddenly I started to panic, as the feeling was not coming back. I tried to force myself to walk and felt my body move forward, then, as if throwing off an old coat, it seemed to fall away from me. I seemed to feel a great relief, then I felt a spinning, then it seemed as if I was travelling as a buzzing energy . . . The next thing I felt as if I had sailed into my own body and as if someone had switched on the light. I was lying on the floor with my mother trying to revive me with water. I got up and was amazed to find I was okay . . ."

(21)   F m 67: ". . . I was back from Theatre in the ward but looking down at myself on the bed. A bottle of blood fell from its stand, blood and confusion and me just looking on. I could hear and see perfectly well all that took place. I was in no pain. I seemed to be above the ME on the bed. I saw doctors and nurses around the bed and heard a doctor say "She is a very bad colour" and another said "She is very cold, Nurse fetch some more blankets". I then decided I should not be out there and tried to get back into my body and found I could not do so. I tried to WILL the doctors to help me. I was mentally telling the doctors to help me. "I AM TRYING, YOU MUST TRY TOO"; this was a great effort and I felt exhausted, however I continued to try. Then I found a place at the top of my head near my forehead where it was possible for me to enter my body. This was the worst part of all. My body seemed to be made of corrugated concrete, if there is such a substance. I will never know how I managed the superhuman effort to get back. Then everything was as normal as after any major operation. While out of my body every detail was perfectly clear to me. I noticed the nurse who was sent for the blankets wore a green dress. When she came to my bed later, I mentioned what had happened, of course she denied that the bottle of blood fell. I told her I knew how it fell. It parted company

with the metal disc that should have held it and the metal disc continued to move backwards and forwards after the bottle fell. The nurse said "We had no time to watch that, believe me" then she said "I *was* the one who fetched the blankets . . ."

All the contributors so far had "out-of-the-body" experiences while lying in bed ((9) — (18)); some of them ill, ((13) — (18)); and the last three while (apparently) unconscious. The next five cases are different —

(22) M 50: ". . . On the 21st March, 1950, I was sitting alone in a room which looked out onto a garden, I was ruminating rather than thinking, when gradually, and quite unexpectedly, I felt myself being borne up a free turning spiral, though my body was, in fact, still well-rooted in the chair . . . . ."

(23) M 49: ". . . Coming home from work on the top deck of a bus about 5 years ago . . . I was in a half-asleep attitude and looking into the woods when I suddenly found myself situated about a hundred yards inside near the trunk of a tree perhaps twelve feet up — when I say situated, I mean *I was* there. I could see and I think hear, because everything was quiet and peaceful. That is although I don't remember any sound I didn't *feel* deaf. But the amazing thing was that I was part of the trees and leaves and nature and that I wasn't anything different. It was most peculiar, I felt this *oneness* . . with everything and had that sympathetic understanding that we were in existence together.

. . . Then suddenly again I was on the bus, no pain, clicks or jerks as smooth a transition back as before when it happened. This experience could have lasted only about 5 or 6 seconds . . ."

Here "out-of-the-body" experience is combined with a feeling of "oneness with everything (1d above)[3]. It is worth noting that, although neither (22) or (23) are lying in bed, one of them is on a bus, their condition is relaxed ("sitting alone, ruminating rather than thinking" (22), and "in a half-asleep attitude" (23)). Quite different are the following three cases —

(24) M 70 (Rev.): ". . . On a very hot day in June 1943 I was

taking a funeral in Brendon, North Devon, for an unknown person in the parish next to mine, as their rector was away. A very badly lighted building. At the end, when leading the bearers down the aisle, at a crossing point, I was suddenly aware of myself in the air doing calculations. So many feet westwards; so many to the north and so many above ground.

This was at the moment when my body did a left turn to go through the arch about 4 yards in front, out to the churchyard. White walls and blazing sun outside. I was saying to myself "I know what they will say — an hallucination due to the contrast between the dark inside and brightness outside. But I have the doorway at an angle of about 20 degrees to the real line of vision if I was on the floor and looking straight through the arch. Also I am looking downwards because I am about 11ft. in the air.

It was this odd experience which made me say it is time to get down to it and try to find out what I am supposed to be doing as a parson. This 18 years after I started parsoning . . ."

The precise topographical details are reminiscent of (23) ("about a hundred yards inside near the trunk of a tree perhaps twelve feet up").

(25) M 90 (Rev.): ". . . When in my early twenties, as a lay preacher, I was taking a service in a tiny village chapel, I had an experience that remains both unusual and unique. Quite without any unusual context, as I carried on the worship, I ceased to be aware of my taking any active part, let alone conducting the service myself. My only experience was that of sitting *behind* myself in the pulpit (noting that I had very square shoulders), whilst I wondered how it came about that I was watching myself conducting the service . . ."

(26) F m 58: ". . . I have been Assistant President of the Girls League and have preached for years and had one wonderful experience of being "out of the body" as I preached . . ."

It is perhaps worth mentioning that people suffering from stage fright sometimes experience a "depersonalised" state in which they do not seem to be speaking and acting themselves but "observing" someone else's doing so.

The next contributor had an "out-of-the-body" experience during prayer, while a nun was saying prayers in the ward where she lay —

> (27) F m 49: ". . . That first night in the ward, one of the nuns knelt down and said the following:—
>
> 'Be present, O merciful Lord, and protect us through the silent hours of this night. So that we, who are wearied by the changes and chances of this fleeting world, may repose upon Thy Eternal Changelessness'.
>
> For the first time, a great peace fell on me; and it seemed to me that "I" was looking down with infinitely tender pity upon this pathetic, crushed, disfigured N.N. (herself); and in that moment of realisation I knew I was no longer identified with her, but was on some entirely different level of consciousness. With the utmost conviction, I *knew* that I was a soul looking at its vehicle, the temporary personality . . ."

It is most interesting that she describes herself as looking down "with infinitely tender pity" at the same time as the prayer is uttered "Be present, O *merciful* Lord, and protect us". She says that she was no longer "identified" with her body: what she does not add is that she was "identifying" herself with the merciful figure who is being addressed (as child does with parent).

So far all the contributors (except (15) by implication) describe their "out-of-the-body" experiences as pleasant (e.g. (13) "joyful beyond anything else I have ever known") or at any rate not unpleasant or frightening. Here is a singular exception —

> (28) F m 62: ". . . I have had one other inexplicable, on the face of it, in sensory terms, experience, but this was the antithesis of religious in any valuable sense; it was what might be described as an experience of limbo or hell and it involved being out of my body and seeing my physical body objectively . . ."

One contributor suggests that he is able to induce "out-of-the-body" experiences at will —

(29) M s 26: ". . . I have been a vegetarian for a year but am relaxing my attitude due to social pressures. I am beginning to be able to project my astral body . . ."

while another practises it in the grand manner, as a means of intercontinental travel —

(30) F m: ". . . I have experienced astral travel when in Melbourne, Australia, back to Market Street, Leicester, where I met someone who was to take on my position in a Diocesan Office here . . ."

— but on these I shall not dwell.

Finally, an experience worth quoting at length, which lasted (on and off) for twenty-four hours, with the writer not only watching her own body in action from outside it, but (unlike our other examples) herself endowed with a duplicate body. The complex emotions she feels towards her "double" are worth noting. (The italics in this account are hers).

(31) F 84: "June 1915. (The war broke up my home near London late in 1914). In January 1915 I went to stay at Tintagel with my children, aged 4 and 5. We lived with the Postman and his wife, lodging with them — Mr. and Mrs. B., half a mile away from the little town. I knew no-one there. The weather was warm and sunny; almost daily I took them to the Church Cliff every afternoon where they played and I occasionally read devotional literature (all I had taken with me: Bible, The Imitation, Prayer book, etc.) and attended church. It was peaceful. The cliffs face west. The sun shone over the sea. Behind, inland, lay a mile of some 15 hedged fields rising gently towards Kingsdown, a low hill with an old 'camp' on it. I got up about 4 p.m. to collect the chicks and their toys to go back for tea round the lane, and look about us. The old church behind us was — I saw — outlined by a stream of golden light. Looking inland I saw every hedge of the 15 fields giving off golden flames, quivering. I stared. Was it my eye-sight? for the June sun was blazing its glittering path across the sea towards us. Then I turned and saw my double, my body, getting up and busying herself with the children, putting them in their little push-chair. She did not see me. I was bewildered. I was her exact duplicate, to her watch-bracelet. I felt myself. I was warm and solid.

'She' presently went off, dawdling and talking to the tinies, and *they* did not see me either. I went along, too, walking independently of them and trying to understand what had happened. They stopped to watch a hedgehog; picked flowers; and I waited nearby for them to go on again. I watcher 'her' closely. I felt some vague jealousy of her, the chicks not missing me; but, at the same time, I was realising an extraordinary happiness, as if all sadness and weariness with our altered circumstances did not matter any more. A great peace filled my mind.

We arrived. Mrs. B. had laid tea. 'She' took the chicks upstairs to tidy and I waited at the foot, hearing it all going on. They came down, sat at the table and Mrs. B. came in with the tray. I hoped that she would see me, for it worried me a little not to be seen by them. But she didn't. I stood, back to the empty fireplace and found I was standing a foot or so above floor level. I could return to the floor. Was I dead? I couldn't be dead. 'She' looked as well as usual. So was I, who felt well as never before. I felt very curious. Routine continued. By 7 p.m. she had put them to bed, I looking on, and come downstairs.

I always went out again, across some fields, by a short cut to the same cliff to watch the sun set and the glorious after glow over the Atlantic, to a stile where I would sit. (A rough slate and turf wall had been passed. She climbed it. I sailed over it, but otherwise I walked.) She perched on the stile and, there being a bit of broken brick wall some way away I went and *leaned up against it*. I could do *that*!

By 9 p.m. we were back at 'our' digs again, in the sitting room where Mrs. B. had lighted an oil lamp. 'She' as usual went out to the kitchen for a glass of milk and a chat with the Bs, who sat at their door looking across their front garden to Kingsdown until they went to bed. But I had to have time to *think*, and stayed in our parlour and sat down. I wondered, am I dying? Will 'she' die in her sleep? If so, I must write three letters. I wrote them, and must evidently have been in my body again, without remarking on it? *I don't know.* What I *do* know is that when 'she' went presently up to bed, I had those letters in my hand. Were they spirit counter parts that I held? The factual letters were on my night table next morning. While she prepared for bed I leant against the window watching her and watching the night roll slowly up from behind Kingsdown. My last recollection.

Next morning Mrs. B. woke me with early tea, and I was in bed. Hastily I covered the letters which I saw on the night table and that was that! I was not dead ('She' was not dead).

It was not the end. Half-way through dressing 'we' separated again. The condition continued all day so that I grew used to it. Eventually we were spending the afternoon again on the cliff. The hedges still flickered with little live golden flames. All was serene. At no time did any persons appear; we had it all to ourselves. It came to 4 p.m. I was standing near them, 'she' busy as on the day before, I looking out to sea, when the glorious light slowly changed and began to dim and it grew ever darker and darker, as if the sun had ceased to shine and night was coming on. But the June sun was still shining out of an unclouded sky, its brilliant path shining over the sea, and 'she' and I were one again. But the sunlight was as a weak candle-glimmer to the light in which I must have been living without knowing it. Back came the sadness and human 'trouble' — things gone that could never come again. It never happened again. Years later when I had Francis Thompson's poems — his 'light invisible, we view thee' — I thought, had he and I seen the same light? . . .

I have read of many persons having seen nature transfigured, the landscape become transcendent. In my case I have seen *nothing* like that. The cliff, church, fields and sea were normal, of earth; the earthly hedges alone *gave off* light, as did the church."

Note first the emotional state preceding the experience — "sadness and weariness with our altered circumstances." As the bodies separate, this changes to "extraordinary happiness", "great peace", "I felt well as never before". Then after the experience "back came the sadness and human 'trouble' ". But happiness and peace were not her only feelings during separation; she was also "bewildered", "very curious", she felt "some vague jealousy" of her double, she had to have "time to think", she wondered "am I dying?" — (cf. 9, 11, 13, 14, 15, 17

78

and 19 above). She remained "separated" from 4 p.m. till bedtime — though she is in some doubt about her condition while writing letters before bed. For next morning the letters were on her bedside table, so she "must evidently have been in my body again, without remarking on it?" — in the morning she "separated" again while dressing, and remained separate till 4 p.m. The experience ended at exactly the same time and place as it had begun the day before. She refers to her body as her "double", for she herself felt "warm and solid" and, though invisible to others, "was her exact duplicate, to her watch-bracelet." — cf. a case recorded by C. Green[4]: "I looked down at my second self and found myself to be a complete replica of my material self. I touched my clothes, and looked at myself and was astounded to see that I was wearing the same black skirt, white blouse with small red spots on it, same shoes, etc. . . . I can remember touching myself and feeling the texture of my clothing; this all felt quite solid . . .". During separation, her double was busy with the children, while she "walked independently", "waited", and "watched"; then she found she was standing "a foot or so above floor level", she "sailed over" a low wall, "leant up against" another wall, and a window, and she wrote three letters. At the time of "separation" there was also a change in the appearance of her surroundings: the hedges and church seemed to give off "golden flames". This illumination ended when the bodies reunited next day, likewise the "extraordinary happiness" and peace.

Chapter 1: e: Notes

1. cf. (30) below.

2. cf. 2c (5) below.

3. Or is it an "out-of-the-body" experience? Perhaps it more properly belongs to 1d, since the writer does not actually mention leaving his body behind (cf. (18) above). On the other hand, the exactness of location of his new viewpoint ("about a hundred yards inside, near the trunk of a tree, perhaps twelve feet up") is not characteristic of "oneness" experiences.

4. *"Out-of-the-Body Experiences"* (Institute of Psycho-Physical Research, Oxford), p. 30.

I: f. TRANSFORMATION OF SURROUNDINGS

We have already met with instances of this in connection with other kinds of experience, e.g. feelings of oneness —

cf. 1d (1)   "... The tree became vibrant, 'real' ..."

(2)   "... Everything becomes suddenly more clearly defined, sights, sounds and smells take on a whole new meaning.. ..."

(8)   "... I had the feeling of seeing the ivy in very sharp focus and then the feeling of everything opening out ..."

(20)   "... everything came alive around about me, and seemed to glow and breathe with animation ..."

Illumination of surroundings (1b above) is one form of transformation. But there are others —

e.g. (1)   F 49: "When I was about twenty, an extraordinary thing happened. Instantly one day *everything changed* before my eyes, all I saw was marvellously and miraculously beautiful. ... I remember I stood there murmuring 'Oh God! Oh God!' Then it faded, leaving a wonderful feeling of joy which lasted several days. For months I tried to recapture it by trying to make conditions outwardly the same (I had been on a small wooded island in a lake, so I used to go into woods, by lakes, etc.) but I have never had it again, or at least with nowhere near such intensity."

(2)   F 29: "... After I was converted, *everything seemed more beautiful to me,* the skies, trees, nature, they all spoke to me of God ..."

(3)   F 41: "... Now I am in harmony with life. The world looks so beautiful in all seasons. It is all so alive, I see every line and detail. It looks as it did when I was an infant ..."

(4)   M 63: "... I was on a walk in Kent on a September day but I was miserable and *the very countryside seemed out of focus* ..."

(5)   F 28: "... I lose track of time and spend maybe 2 or 3 hours just sitting still experiencing a peaceful joyful sort of feeling I seem to become insulated from the outside world — sound, for instance, is not noticeable — and it is only as this feeling

withdraws that I become conscious of my surroundings, which at time *always seem imbued with great beauty, even ordinary objects . . ."*

(6) M 21: ". . . I was grief-stricken and could hardly think. I began to pray very hard for the first time in my life, and as time went on I prayed harder and harder . . . When I finally stopped, *I could hardly recognize the things that were all around for what they had been before.* I was filled with absolute calm . . . and I felt really happy . . ."

(7) F 57: ". . . At the age of 17, out on the moors one day, I suddenly became aware of a different dimension — *everything became intensely vivid* in colouring, and I found a clump of forget-me-nots growing in the middle of a stream, which seemed to be of such blueness that they reflected light. A feeling of well-being and uplifted joy remained when the other feeling passed . . ."

(8) F 56: ". . . After meditating, *sounds are much clearer and solider, so are colours*, and ordinary things look much more interesting . . . I feel less worried and depressed . . ."

(9) M 49[1]: ". . . next morning when I awoke there was an experience which must have lasted possibly the whole day, certainly some hours. *Everything seemed changed,* colour was enhanced and things were so much clearer (rather like 3D) and sounds too. I had never before seen and heard everything so wonderfully well. But also there was a remarkable change in me, a feeling of love and sympathy and one-ness with others which was completely alien . . . There seemed to be an increased quality in all my faculties and perceptions which made everything previous seem grey and dirty . . . But everything returned to normal again after some hours . . ."

(10) M: ". . . When I was about 16 and unhappy at boarding school I suddenly had a flash of intense joy; it only lasted a moment, but I felt that something marvellous was the other side of the nearby hedge, *the whole world seemed physically brighter . . ."*

(11) F 71: ". . . I had been to visit my parents' grave one sunny autumn day. There were patches of blue sky and a light

breeze drove the soft white clouds hither and thither while the sun, shining on a row of yellowing elms, made the leaves look like golden coins as they fluttered noiselessly to the ground. I had seen that view over a period of at least 40 years but on this particular morning *it was completely different.* The sky appeared to open in some strange way and I was able for a brief instant to look through it into another world ... I saw no visions but I felt quite confident I had been given a glimpse of Heaven ... After a few moments I walked away, but when I reached the gate I felt that I must go back again to that same spot and look once more at the sky and the trees. But the experience had passed and I could not recapture it ..."

(12)   F 47: "... I felt as though all the pieces in the mental jigsaw had suddenly fallen into place. I went home quite uplifted, and I remember our very ordinary little garden, there *looking quite different.* The Michaelmas daisies were so brilliant — everything seemed clear and bright and joyful. I don't know how many days I experienced this wonderful lifting up of the spirits ..."

(13)   M 59: "... From 1947 to 1950 I lived with my mother in a stone cottage high up on a hillside, overlooking Blackmore vale. About 12 years later in the early 60's and living then about 40 miles away, I decided to run out and visit this cottage again. My mother had died 3 years back ... A man working in the garden in front of the cottage greeted me and we got into conversation. I informed him that I had lived there some years back. He asked me into the garden and we exchanged information as to what vegetables and flowers grew best in certain positions. As we conversed the situation became unreal. The plants and shrubs and the three pine trees in a copse on the opposite side of the valley became unreal. And yet they were more real than I had ever seen them in the 3½ years I had lived there. Instead of merging into a general familiar picture, *each item of plant, shrub and tree stood out singularly, vivid, vibrant, something on its own apart from the rest.* The whole area became something I had never seen before. I became filled with a feeling of elation and well-being such as I have never before or since experienced. After some half an hour I left the cottage and

walked back to the car. I felt that I had seen Nature as it really is. The feeling of elation and uplift lasted four or five *days* before I finally sank back into my normal attitude..."

(14) F: "... The Isle of Man ... it was sunny, warm and quiet. The rustle of corn, deep blue of the sky and glinting sea affected me profoundly. I felt both complete and non-existent. *The colours* were clearer and everything was 'right'. I lost myself in it all. Absolute peace ..."

We may note certain common features. The change in appearances is always associated with a change in the person's *feelings,* usually to joy or elation —

cf. (1) "... a wonderful feeling of joy ..."

(2) "... in harmony with life ..."

(5) "... a peaceful joyful sort of feeling ..."

(6) "... I was filled with absolute calm and I felt really happy ..."

(7) "... a feeling of well-being and uplifted joy ..."

(10) "... a flash of intense joy ..."

(12) "... uplifted ..."

(13) "... a feeling of elation and well-being ..."

But sometimes the change goes the other way, towards depression, and then the surroundings, instead of growing bright and beautiful, ("each item ... singularly vivid, vibrant ..."), seem uniformly grey and dreary —

e.g. (4) "... I was miserable and the very countryside seemed out of focus ..."

Most writers assume it is the change in appearance that *causes* the change in their feelings, or at least that the latter is secondary —

cf. (1) "... it faded, leaving a wonderful feeling ..."

(7) "... A feeling of well-being and uplifted joy remained ..."

(9) "... also there was a remarkable change in me ..."

But a few, perhaps more perceptive, put it the other way round, writing of —

"a sense of exhilaration which *made* the day suddenly brighten" (2c (4) below),

"illumination of mind so *subjectively* vivid that I fancied a change even in the light around me",

or how "almost ecstatic wonder . . . from time to time blazes up and *illuminates everything around* with an incredible beauty."

An extreme case is that of John Custance[2] who writes:

"My last manic episode . . . began nearly a year ago, with the usual curious change in sense-perception of the outer world. I can only describe it by saying that "the lights go up", as if a kind of switch were turned in my psycho-physical system. Everything seems different, somehow brighter and clearer . . . It is quite easily recognizable and bitter experience has now taught me that, as soon as it occurs, I should take immediate steps to go to hospital, since within a few days I shall be out of control . . ."

The influence of mood on surroundings can be to make them seem friendly —

cf. 1a (15) ". . . The sky, flowers, trees and even the grass were pulsing with friendliness . . ."

1a (17) ". . . the shadows of the house and trees seemed friendly and protective . . ."

2d (2) ". . . I must have drifted into an exalted state. The moon . . . seemed to have become personalised and observant . . . the pleasant resinous odour (of balsam poplars) conveyed goodwill . . . The river . . . was now concerned with my return . . ."

— or hostile —

cf. 1a (1) ". . . a sense of overpowering evil . . . a malign presence so tangible that it was endowed with something like shape . . . . ."

or Proust[3]

". . . the hostility of the violet curtains and the insolent indifference of a clock that chattered on at the top of its voice as though I were not there . . ."

85

The phrase "paranoid projection" has become a layman's commonplace, implying the unconscious attribution of one's own (repressed) hostility to one's surroundings.

Cyril Connolly[4] speculates: "In manic elation communication seems to exist between inanimate objects and the 'observer'. Flowers signal to him, stones cry out, and all nature approves. In suicidal depression the same phenomena arise, but in this case nature seems to pass a vote of censure; inanimate objects urge the 'Observer' to make a good job of it. Are both fatigue and ecstasy poisons which distort our relation to our surroundings? Or do they liberate deep-buried instinctive perceptions of relationships to which normally we are blind?"

In our own examples the sudden flash of elation often follows a period of anxiety or depression —

e.g. 1d(20) "I had been under very great emotional strain . . . and this had become extreme in the immediately preceding months."

2d   (2) ". . . a mood of depression had come down . . ."; then "I must have drifted into an exalted state . . ."

       (6) ". . . I was grief-stricken . . ."

       (10) ". . . unhappy at boarding school . . ."

What induces the sudden change of mood? Sometimes, as with Custance above, it seems to be a spontaneous swing (common with manic-depressives), and cf. 1d (20) and 2d (2) — "I had been forced back into myself . . . and could go no further; when this happened I think there was an equally extreme reaction . . .". For (2), it was the effect of religious conversion, for (9), of a church service, for (5) and (8), of meditation, for (6), of prayer, and (15), of reconversion —

(15) M 78: ". . . Upon a grassy bank I stood lost in troubled, despondent brooding at this departure of religious belief. What then occurred at this point is not easily put into words. There was a sudden freeing within, and a swift indescribable illumination of mind, so subjectively vivid that I fancied a change even in the light around me. A deep sigh beneath this experience, an involuntary gaze upward, and I then became conscious of an exquisite sense of relief and peace. My

gloomy doubts had been instantly swept away by this mysterious inrush, leaving behind a new deep belief in the existence of God and in the complete truth of Christian doctrine, and a greatly widened vision of, and revived longing for, goodness as an ideal of life. I recollect that as I walked homeward through the bustling streets, and passed the busy shops and clanging electric cars, all the familiar environment seemed charged with a new joyousness and happy zest . . ."

Duration

How long does the transformation last? It varies —

(9) ". . . some hours . . ."

(10) ". . . it only lasted a moment . . ."

(11) ". . . a few moments . . ."

(12) ". . . days . . ."

Often — e.g. (1), (7) and (9) — the elation persists long after the change in appearances has faded. The fortunate (3), however, seems permanently to view her surroundings with the eye of innocence, to see them "apparelled in celestial light".

Lastly, I think it is worth distinguishing three different kinds of experience that involve a change in relations with one's surroundings. The different kinds may occur together or separately. First, there is the change in appearance that we have just discussed: "everything seemed more real, vibrant", "things came alive", "the moon comforted me", "the tree looked hostile, angry", etc. Secondly, there is the feeling of "oneness" described in 1d above: "I felt part of it all", "I seemed to melt into the trees", etc. Thirdly, we have a great many statements like this — "I felt awe in that silent numinous place." Now this need not imply any change in appearances, but it often does imply something else — the feeling of a presence of some kind —

cf. 1a (16) ". . . I was aware of Something 'within' and 'behind' the mere flowers . . . Something smiles and salutes and recognises me . . ."

This sense of "presence" I shall discuss in Chapter 5.

Chapter 1: f: Notes

1. cf. 1e (22).
2. *Adventure into the Unconscious* (Christopher Johnson, 1954).
3. *Swann's Way,* Part 1.
4. Palinurus: *The Unquiet Grave* (Hamish Hamilton).

CHAPTER 2

AUDITORY EXPERIENCE

"Voices". — These we can divide into roughly two kinds: (a) comforting, reassuring "voices", and (b) guiding "voices", commands. Within each kind we can further distinguish between 1. the "voice of God" (or of some other unidentified Being), and 2. the "voices" of familiar people, usually recently dead, addressing the bereaved.

*　　*　　*　　*　　*

a) Comforting "voices"

1. *"Voice of God" (or of some other unidentified Being).*

We mentioned the absurdity of the idea of "overhearing" the voice of God address somebody else. It would be no less odd to imagine hearing such a voice address oneself on some quite impersonal topic, such as the weather. As with visions, the relation with the voice is an *affective* one. In this section people unhappy or under stress hear "comfortable words".

Three contributors heard a "voice" calling them *by name:*

(1) F m 55: ". . . Gradually I became aware of this power and began to really court it. It has come to me often — once in a dream — as light, warmth, comfort and love past understanding. It has walked with me and sometimes I hear *something or someone calling my name.*"

For her this became a familiar occurrence; the next contributor experienced it only once, and unlike the others, was not feeling troubled at the time —

(2) F m 48: "On 18th April, 1958 I had what is best described as a 'Samuel' experience[1]. I was not under stress or disturbed, nor was the day in any way unusual. We lived in Northern Uganda, and had just started on our second tour — the first

one had been very difficult with money troubles and a premature baby — but now everything, including the baby, was improving. This particular day my three small girls were sleeping and my husband was out. It was about 2-3 p.m. and suddenly I *felt my name* — no voice — but such a sensation of something calling me that I moved to my bedroom. Automatically I knelt by the bed. There wasn't any great revelation — but my reaction was to want to pray, perhaps four or five times a day to try to reach this 'power' — and it was a power of righteousness and cleansing — it made me search my behaviour."

(3)   F s 74: ". . . My 'spiritual' experience came when I was 33. I had just been jilted by one whom I trusted, and could not feel that life held anything for me. I had no suicidal tendencies, but found myself walking in the middle of a busy road. A voice (or a "Voice") said to me quite distinctly 'Stella, Stella, go to the pavement' and I found myself there. Since then I have, I think, been able to be of help and of use in the world. I am extremely happy and have many blessings. Although I live alone I am never lonely. When the curtains are drawn and work done I often experience a deep sense of peace . . ."

Several people heard a "voice" telling them to relax. These two heard it in answer to prayer —

(4)   F m 60: ". . . Once in a dentist's chair, my stomach and bowels seemed to go on a rampage . . . I started to pray; suddenly I heard and felt an authoritative voice in the centre of my head say 'Relax'. Instantly the discomfort stopped. I was able to smile and converse when the dentist came to work on me . . ."

(5)   F s 64: ". . . When I was abroad and living under great stress, I had the experience of a voice that seemed apart from me: 'I don't want your prayers — relax your body and spirit in my presence' . . ."

Another spoke of *repeatedly* ". . . hearing in times of great stress a voice with the ability to soothe and calm."

For the next two, the "message" took the form of an assurance that they were in God's care —

(6) F s 54: "At one time I reached utter despair and wept and prayed God for mercy instinctively and without faith in reply. That night I stood with other patients in the grounds waiting to be let in to our ward. It was a very cold night with many stars. Suddenly someone stood beside me in a dusty brown robe and a voice said 'Mad or sane, you are one of My sheep'. I never spoke to anyone of this but ever since, twenty years, it has been the pivot of my life. I realise that the form of the vision and the words I heard were the result of my education and cultural back-ground but the voice, though closer than my own heartbeat, was entirely separate from me."

(7) F s: "Just over a year ago I returned to Thailand after a year at home on leave. Quite a bit of furlough I spent worrying about all the problems that could arise during these coming years (and quite a few of them have already arisen...). Then I came the nearest to an inner voice that I've ever been when I suddenly had this warmth of heart as it seemed God spoke to me. 'Your times are in my hand. I've been in control of this situation and I can control situations in North Thailand so you don't need to fear.' Suffice it to say that I returned in a very different state of mind without any further delay at home. I've certainly had opportunity during this year of putting that claim to the test, and have found that God has been true to his Word."

"You don't need to fear"[2] was also the gist of the message heard by several other contributors —

e.g. (8) F m 49: "I was 'converted', overnight, after a night of vivid dreams — also healed of migraine after three years' misery.. I also heard the words 'Be not afraid' after hearing a rapping on my window."

For two contributors there was the assurance that "everything" would be all right" —

(9) M 70 (Dr.): "Once in direst distress, no way out, Jesus sat beside me in my car and said 'Do not look at me. All will be well'."

(10) F m 23: "... The strangest thing that ever happened was when I was about 16. A friend of mine had been taken ill at

the beginning of the week and towards the end of that same week while getting dressed one morning, I decided to kneel in front of a small cross I had in my room and say a quick prayer — I seemed to find myself in a great hall without walls or a roof. I was kneeling down on something quite firm and yet I was not conscious of a floor. I had a feeling of great rushing winds and yet everything was quite still and silent. Everything was grey like a summer morning early, shrouded in mist waiting to burst into life. Before me was a presence clothed in mist. Omnipotent. I was not conscious of good or evil, joy or pain, fear or relief. Somehow, in a still small voice that penetrated my being, like the loudest noise in the universe, I was told that 'Everything is going to be all right'."

Two others were comforted by the same words quoted from the Bible —

(11) M 75 (Rev.): ". . . When I was middle-aged and the 2nd World War upon us, there came a night when I was in deepest distress of mind. I was alone in my bedroom, pacing the floor . . . Suddenly, I heard a voice firmly say 'Be still and know that I am God!' It changed my life. I got into bed, calm and confident. Confidence 'possessed' me day after day . . ."

(12) F m 49: "When my first husband died in Mombasa I was in a fearful state, through shock after his long illness . . . Some clear voice said 'Be still and know that I am God' — I was."

A child writes:—

(13) F: "I was sitting by the fire, head in hand, worrying about it, and I said to myself and God 'I still haven't done much to prove I love mankind' and, before I'd finished that sentence in my mind, these few words came, as it were, through the opposite way . . . 'Well you've proved it to me anyway'."

Certain points are worth noting:
Mood just before the experience —

(3) ". . . jilted . . . could not feel that life held anything for me."

(4) ". . . my stomach and bowels seemed to go on a rampage."

(5) ". . . under great stress."

(6) ". . . reached utter despair."

(7) ". . . worrying . . ."

(8) ". . . three years' misery . . ."

(9) ". . . in direst distress. . ."

(11) ". . . in deepest distress. . ."

(12) ". . . in a fearful state . . ."

(13) ". . . worrying . . ."

Only (2) particularly states that she was "not under stress or disturbed", and for her the effect of hearing her name called was not so much comforting as a spur to action. (1) was concerned not about herself but a friend[3] and the experience brought neither "fear or relief."

Nature of "voice" —
Seven said straightforwardly "I heard a voice" or "a voice said". But four described it as an "inner" voice, or not even a voice —

(2) ". . . suddenly I *felt* my name — no voice — but such a *sensation* of something calling me . . ."

(4) ". . . suddenly I heard and *felt* an authoritative voice *in the centre of my head* say . . ."

(7) ". . . I came the nearest to an *inner* voice that I've ever been . . .".

(13) ". . . in my mind, these few words came, as it were, through the opposite way . . ."

whereas

(5) ". . . had the experience of a voice that *seemed* apart from me".

and (6) though a paradox, has it both ways —
". . . the voice, though closer than my own heartbeat[4], was entirely separate from me."

This contrast between "inner" and "outer" voices exactly parallels that in 1b above (p. 15) where some "felt" "inner" light, and others "saw" light outside themselves. (10) resorts extensively to paradox — ". . . a still small voice that penetrated my being like the loudest noise in the universe" (cf. "a . . . hall without walls or a roof", "great rushing winds and yet everything was still and silent"). (6) and (9) both say the speaker appeared "*beside* me", not face-to-face as is usual in non-speaking visions (p. 3 above). One tends to adopt this position when trying to console someone with words (or touch).

Emotional accompaniment —
Note (7) "I suddenly had this warmth of heart as it seemed God spoke to me . . ." The warmth does not appear to *follow* the hearing of the words as a separable effect, but to accompany them; it is part of the experience — its "affective tone" (cf. 2c (4) below ". . . *accompanied* by a sense of exhilaration . . ."). We need not particularise about the comfort and reassurance felt by the other contributors. Sudden change of mood is basic to the experience.

2. *"Voice from the dead."*

Just as a large proportion of visions were of a dead person "appearing" to the bereaved, usually to comfort them (1a, p. 6 above), so in more than half the accounts of hearing a comforting "voice" somebody recently dead "spoke" to the bereaved. The gist of the message was usually "Don't grieve for me", "I'm all right" or "I'm with you".

e.g. (14) F w: ". . . My husband passed on after much suffering in 1937. Within 24 hours of his passing came the most wonderful experience I have ever had, for I felt him beside me, so happy and so full of life and vitality, where before he had been so dreadfully weak . . . I never doubted from that moment that there is no death. I saw nothing, but I definitely sensed his presence and this continued for six months, for whenever I felt sad and the tears came, almost instantly he would say 'Don't cry, I am still with you'. I would look all around the room and say 'Where are you, I know you are here', but I never have seen him."

(15) M 81 (Major): ". . . IN 1961 I lost by death a friend who had been very close to me since 1914 . . . One day I was looking at a magnificent display of roses, and said sadly: 'How I wish

you could see these roses which you helped to plant!' The answer formed itself most clearly and unexpectedly in my mind: 'But I *can* see them quite well, through your eyes!'. . ."

(16) M 48 (Lt. Col.): ". . . What I am about to write to you is something which I have experienced at intervals since 1939. To put it in the simplest terms it is this: after the death of someone I know, I get a clear and definite impression of their visiting me, two three or four days after their death, to tell me that, so to speak, they are all right. I cannot say whether this experience occurs when I am thinking of them or whether it comes uninvited. I first recall it in 1939 after my grandfather died, and I last experienced it in February of this year after I had been to the funeral of an acquaintance (as distinguished from a close friend). . . With one exception which I shall come to later, the impression given is that they are content, and the time taken for the happening to occur seems to be in proportion to the degree in which I have known the dead person. For example, I mentioned above the acquaintance whose funeral I attended in February. I remember not being in communication with him for four days and then only fleetingly. Others whom I have known better have got in touch earlier and stayed in touch longer (I am talking in terms of seconds and minutes). The only occasion when this experience was not a contented one concerned a doctor whom I knew reasonably well in Cyprus. He was a Regimental Medical Officer and was shot by the terrorists. I did not go to the funeral and I had the most clear impression that he was in great distress. This is not the sort of thing one talks about and I was, therefore, surprised when the Padre (C of E or Church of Wales) told me that he had the same impression in a more dramatic and distressing form . . . This is not an easy matter to write about if only because our language seems inadequate to describe a spiritual sensation."

(17) F m 87: ". . . I was walking down the country lane to the church yard where my son was buried. He walked with me all the way till I got to where I left the road and went to his grave. When I got back to the lane he came again and said

95

'Mummy, I am here with you', until I got home . . ."

(18) F s: ". . . one morning a telephone message called me home as my father had died suddenly . . . On the boat I decided to get away from everyone and go on to the top deck. As the boat got under way, gulls flew round in the sunlight in circling formation. It was then, over the Irish Sea, that I heard, though not in a physical sense, my father's voice in an unusually high and exultant tone calling to me on the wind 'I am free'. This unusual experience was particularly comforting . . ."

(19) F w 77: ". . . My husband died 19 years ago when I was 58 years old. I was tearful, still I suppose in a state of shock, and haunted by incidents, in the near past particularly, when I could have been more sensitive to his needs, more understanding, in fact more loving. The service of Matins proceeded until we came to the Collect for the day (21st after Trinity) in which we prayed for pardon and peace, for cleansing and a quiet mind. The familiar words came to me with great impact as exactly meeting my needs, and as I accepted God's forgiveness, I was aware of my husband's presence with me and he was saying 'And I forgive you too, and there are things for which I need your forgiveness' and then he said 'Live close to God and I shall be near you'. I can't describe the vividness of this experience. I saw nothing, and nothing was audible, and yet all this was conveyed to me . . ."

(20) M s 73: ". . . Probably a year after he passed on, I was awakened in the middle of the night by a very urgent summons calling my name 'N-N'. I remember springing out of bed and landing on my feet, and there in front of me was my friend, in the same golden light that I had witnessed with the vision of my mother. Not a word was spoken but the eyes seemed to say to me 'There is life after death'. The strange thing about this is that I have the strongest feeling that I witnessed the vision of my friend with my material eyes closed . . ."

(21) F m 70: ". . . My brother was killed on June 16th, 1915 . . . I was beyond human help. My loved brother came back . . . He said (I did not hear with my ears, but with my

intelligence) 'Why are you grieving like this? If it is for me, you need not' . . ."

Contrast the following —

(22) F m 54: ". . . About four years ago, my neighbour, a young woman of thirty-eight years, died. The day of the funeral I was at business, working as usual; suddenly it flashed in my mind, clear, the hearse was passing her house on the way to church. She came out of the hearse, walked into the house, looked around, touched the table-tops, turned to me and said 'N —, it was not worth worrying about material things and home, I should have spent more time spiritually', and with that went right back to the hearse . . ."

Here we have something different in kind from all the preceeding. There seems to be no affective side to the experience at all; no mention of grief, bereavement or comfort from the words of the departed. Instead we have matter-of-fact details ("she came out of the hearse, walked into the house, looked round, touched the table-tops", etc.), reminiscent of the details in 1a (1), or 1c (16) — (18), above. As with these, I should wish to distinguish it from a "religious", or even "spiritual" experience.

Now to particularise:

Mood, etc. just before the experience —

(14) ". . . whenever I felt sad".

(15) ". . . said sadly . . ."

(17) ". . . walking down the country lane to the churchyard where he was buried" (cf. (1) and (3) above, who were also walking at the time).

(18) ". . . decided to get away from everyone . . ."

(19) ". . . tearful . . . in a state of shock . . ."

Nature of voice

Here, as with the "voice" of God (and cf. I:b. above on "light"), we have a division between "inner" & "outer". Three contributors say straightforwardly that somebody spoke. Now consider the rest —

(15) ". . . The answer *formed itself* most clearly and unexpectedly in my mind . . ."

(16) ". . . language seems inadequate to describe a *spiritual sensation*".

(17) ". . . I heard, though *not in a physical sense* . . ."

(19) ". . . nothing was audible . . ."

(21) ". . . not . . . with my ears, but with my intelligence".

Note also the non-verbal communication in

(20) ". . . Not a word was spoken, but the eyes seemed to say to me . . ."

Accompanying "sense of presence".

(14) ". . . I felt him beside me[5] . . . definitely sensed his presence . . . but I have never seen him . . ."

(16) ". . . a clear and definite impression of their visiting me . . . a spiritual sensation . . ."

(17) ". . . He walked with me . . ."

(19) ". . . I was aware of my husband's presence with me . . . saw nothing, but . . . he seemed nearer to me than in life. . ."[6]

(20) ". . . have the strongest feeling that I witnessed the vision of my friend with my material eyes closed . . ."

The emotional impact need not be emphasised — "I have never doubted from that moment", "particularly comforting", "it dried my tears", etc.

b) "Voices", guiding

1. *A "call"*

This is very frequent in the Bible, a common formula being "The Word of the Lord came unto me, saying 'Do Y.' "

(1)   F s 75: ". . . I had to consider what to do next. Then came my call. A voice said to me in English 'Go to Jerusalem'. This was repeated three times 'Go to Jerusalem, Go to Jerusalem' in mounting tones . . . I remained there for fiteen years — the happiest years of my long life."

(2)   M s 55: ". . . I was kneeling quietly before the altar, feeling such a wondrous peace enfolding me, when suddenly I was startled by three loud 'cracks' above the altar, like three slow hand claps. Then a Voice, not audible in the air, but a deep insistent inner Voice said 'Now, my son, your day has come. I want you to open a Sanctuary of Divine Healing by Prayer . . .'"

(3)   M 50: ". . . In the ensuing silence a voice spoke and said "Take forth my Word". This was not a physical voice, nor an imaginary voice, but the voice of God. Let me try and describe how it seemed to utter itself. It was as though I was the sounding board, or perhaps I should say the magnetic tape, and the Heavens above used the very energy which had raised me beyond myself to play the 'tape' — my own inner self. It was an occasion full of awe . . ."

2. *What some might simply call the 'voice of conscience'.*

(4)   M 80: ". . . As regards my personal contact with the unseen, since the age of fifteen I have had an ever-recurring sense of a voice saying 'This is the way, walk ye in it'. Obedience to it has always led to happiness . . ."

(6)   F m 61: ". . . After Communion Service on Sunday evening I went to light up a cigarette on arriving home when a voice inside me said 'You don't really need that, you know'. To myself I said 'Don't be silly'. Then I thought 'That's funny. I wonder if it's true'. I decided I'd see. I put the cigarette out — kept the remainder of the packet for months, but never once had the desire to smoke again . . ."

(7)   F s (Nun): "All through my life He has communicated with my spirit and on many occasions when circumstances have called for it, I have heard His voice. Clear words have been given me and spoken in a tone of undoubted authority, yet personal, warm, and, as it were, belonging . . ."

3. *What some might simply call a "sixth sense".*

These examples remind one of Socrates' warning "daimon", except that this only told him what *not* to do.

(8)   F m 63: "Driving along a country road in Somerset, behind a heavy lorry, I heard a voice (woman's?) call 'Look out!' I said to my husband 'Who called Look Out?' He said 'No-

one. This is a desolate road!' I had slowed down immediately; the voice was clear and urgent. The lorry in front suddenly swerved across the road and stopped, blocking it completely. The driver had fallen asleep. If I had not heard that voice I should have been passing it at that instant . . ."

(9) M m 26: ". . . I was travelling to work in my car when I suddenly became very cold. I then heard a voice which seemed to come from inside me, and the voice said 'Oh son, don't go so fast!' Then I felt arms gripping me tightly. I was so shocked by this, I immediately braked, and before I had come to a halt, a car came round the corner towards me, travelling at a terrific speed and heading straight for me. The car swerved violently in order to miss my car, and only just avoided a collision . . . I recognised the voice as belonging to my aunt who passed away ten years ago; she always called me 'son' . . ."

(10) M 83 (Rev.): "Accepted for the Canadian Methodist Church; experiences of bitter cold; hearing a voice in a prolonged blizzard 'Horse-sense!' led me to drop the reins, and my horse, with its amazing sense, saved my life. To me it was the voice of God."

(11) F m 44 (member of Yugoslav Resistance, describing wartime escape): ". . . On the way, a voice told me to pretend going in, that is, open the door, go around the outhouse, jump over the fence . . . The 'voice' was not a birth of my tortured mind to find a way out; but rather like a person all of a sudden remembering a word or an instant years ago, without even thinking or trying to remember . . ."

As to the nature of the "voice" — for some, it seemed to come from "outside" —

e.g. (5) ". . . I looked round to see if anyone was near — the 'voice' seemed to come from right beside me . . ."[7]

— or "beside me", cf. 2a (6), (9) & (18).

(8) ". . . I said to my husband 'Who called, Look out?' "

— but nobody was visible in either case.

For most, the "voice" was an "inner" one —

(2) ". . . not audible in the air, but a deep insistent inner Voice".

(3) ". . . not a physical voice . . . it seemed to utter itself . . . as though I was the sounding board, or perhaps I should say the magnetic tape, and the Heavens above used the very energy which had raised me beyond myself, to play the 'tape' — my own inner self."

This is an interesting description. On "seemed to utter itself", cf. 2c below (being spoken through); but in this case, although the writer himself felt he uttered the words, he was "being addressed" in the second person.[8]

The connection between a high level of arousal ("the very energy which had raised me above myself") and the hearing of "voices", seeing of "visions", "lights", etc. I discuss elsewhere. It ties up with what I have already stressed — the affective basis of such experiences; cf. 2c (5), where there is an *accompanying* (not just ensuing) "sense of *exhilaration* which made the day suddenly brighten", or 1a (15), "more real than the Light itself was the unbearable *ecstasy* that accompanied it", or 2a (7). Here, too, "it was an occasion full of *awe*".

(6) ". . . a voice inside me said . . ."

(7) ". . . heard a voice in my mind say . . ."

(9) ". . . heard a voice that seemed to come from inside myself . . ."

But she also "recognised the voice as belonging to my aunt who passed away ten years ago"[9], and at the same time "felt arms gripping me tightly", an excellent example of the indistinctness between "inner" and "outer" "objects" in these experiences.

(12) ". . . The 'voice' was . . . rather like a person all of a sudden remembering a word or an instant years ago, without even thinking or trying to remember . . ."

This is an excellent description of what seems to happen "automatically"; cf. 2a (14) ". . . The answer formed itself most clearly and unexpectedly in my mind", and 2c (being spoken through) passim.

c) "Being spoken through"

(1) M s (55): ". . . the Father told me to make no notes and to know that He would give me the words I had to speak. It was then that the next important experience came to me. As I stood up to speak, all nervousness disappeared in a great peace, and a sentence formed in my mind — then another, until I found I had but to repeat the words."

(2) F m 67: ". . . If at any time emotion tends to make me try to help someone with words, at times they seem to come as it were independently. These words tend to find their mark."

(3) M s 38: "About six years ago there occurred a series of events unique in my life. For a period of days — even weeks — I felt strangely 'withdrawn' from my surroundings, but at the same time elated and excited. One evening, while visiting friends (who later described my behaviour as 'like one drugged'), I found myself uttering the following words: 'Everything is relative . . . It's all a matter of degree . . . Love without touching; don't touch without loving". These words puzzled me at the time, and still do. It was as if I was *repeating*, without understanding, something that was being said to me . . ."

(4) M 54: ". . . Just before the outbreak of war in 1939 I was in considerable perplexity and spiritual torment. I hated the prospect of the approaching conflict and had become convinced that Christian Pacifism was the right course to follow, even at the cost of defeat and death . . . One Saturday morning at about 10 o'clock I was walking through the town, not consciously occupied with this problem, when at a precise spot I could point out, there burst on me a clear exclamation 'It is for me! It is for me!' This was in verbal form and accompanied by a sense of exhilaration which made the day suddenly brighten. I understood this as meaning I was personally assured of inclusion in God's love and that however difficult the decision I had to take, or its consequences, He would be with me. . ."

These accounts have much in common:

(1) ". . . a sentence formed in my mind" (cf. 2a (14) "the answer formed itself . . . in my mind") ". . . I had but to repeat the words. . ."

102

(2) ". . . they seemed to come as it were independently. . ."

(3) ". . . It was as if I was repeating . . . something that was being said to me . . ."

(4) ". . . there burst upon me a clear exclamation . . ."

Note also the affective state —

(1) ". . . all *nervousness* disappeared in a great peace. . ."

(2) ". . . any time *emotion* tends to make me try . . ."

(3) ". . . strangely 'withdrawn' from my surroundings, but at the same time *elated* and *excited* . . ."

(4) ". . . a sense of *exhilaration* . . . that banished perplexity and spiritual torment . . ."

The experience of *being spoken through*[10] happens commonly with mediums, who often speak with the "voices" of those who are "communicating" "from the other side". Similarly with ancient oracles, e.g. the Delphic oracle, where the priest or priestess would go into a trance (it was essentially an emotional phenomenon) and speak with the god's "voice" by whom they were temporarily "possessed". "Speaking with tongues" is a related phenomenon.

Here is a less dramatic example from the Church of England —

(5) F m 60: ". . . I feel God is speaking through me. When I take a service, my own personality is something secondary to the feeling that I am a kind of medium through which God is trying to reach the congregation . . ."

What applies to speaking can also apply to writing. An Indian scientist writes:

(6) M s: ". . . These poems have all been as if from "Somebody Else" and not my own. I write them only as and when they come, so that I am only at the receiving end of 'Somebody' whom I dimly know . . ."

"Automatic" writing is a common practice among mediums. Romantic poets invoke their "Muse", and, like prophets, await the moment of "inspiration".

What applies to speaking and writing can even apply to

103

playing the piano —

    (7) M m 44: ". . . I was alone in my studio playing through a Chopin Sonata which I had played quite often in public. The piece was very much 'in my fingers'. I was also tired but excited and moved by the music. Suddenly I found I was listening like an audience and the 'doing' seemed to be 'being done' through me . . ."

Indeed, there was recently a case where a lady, Rosemary Brown, apparently not an accomplished musician, claimed to be "played through" by a variety of long-dead composers, and certainly improvised works remarkably similar to their styles.

4. *"Music" and other "noises"*.

    (1) M 74 (Dr.): April 1917, France; battalion resting briefly from trenches —

"While spending an afternoon hour alone in my hill-top wood, a mood of depression had come down. We were due to move in a few days. The background of winter ought to have made easy an unvarying response to this ideal place. But that afternoon responsiveness had been lacking. After supper in the mess I felt restless. I wondered if the full moon shining down from a cloudless sky had anything to do with my mood. A walk by the canal might make it easier to sleep. I walked eastward for about two miles along the tow-path and then turned about. The nearer I drew to the village, the more alive my surroundings seemed to become. It was as if something which had been dormant when I was in the wood were coming to life. I must have drifted into an exalted state. The moon, when I looked up at it, seemed to have become personalised and observant, as if it were aware of my presence on the tow-path. A sweet scent pervaded the air. Early shoots were breaking from the sticky buds of the balsam poplars which bordered the canal; their pleasant resinous odour conveyed good-will. The slowly moving waters of the canal, which was winding its unhurried way from the battle-fields to the sea, acquired a 'numen' which endorsed the intimations of the burgeoning trees. The river conveyed that it had seen me before in other places and knew something about me. It was now concerned with my return to the village[12]. But I couldn't decide whether my movement along the tow-path was being encouraged or hindered. A feeling that I was being absorbed into the living surroundings gained in intensity and was working up to a climax. Something was going to happen. Then it happened. The experience lasted, I should say, about thirty seconds and seemed to come out of the sky in which were resounding majestic harmonies. The thought: 'That is the music of the spheres'[13] was immediately followed by a glimpse of luminous bodies — meteors or stars — circulating in predestined courses emitting both light and music. I stood still on the tow-path and wondered if I was going to fall down. I dropped on to one knee and thought: How wonderful to die at this moment. I put a hand over my forehead as if to contain the tumult and fend off something. Wonder, awe, and gratitude mounted to a climax and remained poised for a few seconds like a German star shell. Then began the foreknown descent. The revolving flares in the sky were extinguished; the orchestration faded into silence; the river and its guarding poplars lost their magic. And the moon, which was still shining exactly the same place overhead, regained its impersonal detachment. I got on to my feet and the thought came: Get back to your room and get into bed. You can think about all this tomorrow. In a dazed state I found my way to my billet. The mess was empty, the others having dispersed. When I looked at my wristwatch I saw that the hour was late. It was after two..."

Apart from the "music" (and accompanying "vision"), this account is rich in details typical of many: there is the prior depression, changing into "an exalted state"; at the same time the surroundings seemed to become "alive", the moon "personalised and observant" "aware of my presence", the smell of the balsam poplars "conveyed good-will", the river was "concerned" about his return. On the connection between emotional state and appearance of surroundings, cf. 2c (4) "a sense of exhilaration which made the day suddenly brighten". And on seeing things as "You's", cf. 1a (11) — (20). The "exalted state" turns to "wonder, awe and gratitude" ("I dropped on to one knee", "I put a hand over my forehead"), and after the experience he remains "in a dazed state".

And now for something completely different —

(2) F s 42: "... Last Saturday I went to bed mid-morning for a

necessary rest. I had a vision in colour of the first wife of the widower minister I am now sure is going to ask me to marry him quite soon. She smiled, and the smile encouraged me to make a decision that, basically, I very much wanted to make, a decision to go to hear him preach. Everything in that dream-vision is explicable in psychological terms but one thing, the powder-blue, deepish, of the suit she wore . . . In these restful moments on the Friday evening, I am, though tired, able to distinguish the wavelength noises, not tinnitus, in my ears — I've been conscious of them for some time. The broad low-pitched sound I connect with the gentleman who is, I hope, going to ask me to marry him. The rather sombre, at-intervals, keen-edged yet also low-pitched noise I attribute to his university friend, a rather sombre person with tendencies towards gloom — this man is also, now, a from-time-to-time discussion-companion of my own, and a minister also. The high-pitched, fairly frequent tone belongs to a Roman Catholic priest who knows both N — and me and is good enough to be concerned, without worrying about me. He is, I believe, a good authority, a very fine preacher as well as an excellent school-teacher and priest. The rather abrupt, very occasional strong tone I attribute to the priest's canon, a very worthy gentleman indeed with much knowledge of life . . ."

Chapter 2: Notes

1. cf. Samuel 1.3: ". . . the Lord called 'Samuel' . . . and the Lord called yet again 'Samuel' . . . and the Lord called 'Samuel' again the third time . . . And the Lord . . . called as at other times 'Samuel, Samuel' " (cf. Samuel 3.1: "The word of the Lord was precious in those days; there was no open vision.")

2. cf. St. Luke 1, where the "angel of the Lord" says to Zacharias "Fear not, Zacharias: for thy prayer is heard . . ."; to Mary "Fear not, Mary: for thou hast found favour . . ."; and to the shepherds "Fear not: for behold I bring you good tidings . . ."

3. See 1c. p. 37 for other cases where concern for another triggers off a "sensory" experience.

4. cf. Upanishads, "Closer is He than breathing . . ." "closer to me than I am to myself."

5. "Beside me", cf. note on 2a (6) & (9), p. 94.

6. cf. The poem "Possession" by John Freeman:
   And I see you
   And I hold you:
   But are you yet living,
   Or come you now nearer than any man living may be?

7. cf. Samuel's mistaking God's voice for Eli's (I. Sam., 1:3, 5-8).

8. cf. the following: F m: ". . . While lying on my bed in meditation . . . I could hear her voice *in my throat.*"

9. The only "voice from the dead" occurring in this section; contrast 2a.

10. See note 2 to p. 102.

11. Note the emotional state: ". . . tired but excited and moved . . ."; cf. (3) ". . . 'withdrawn' but at the same time elated and excited".

12. cf. quotation from C. Connolly, p. 86 above.

13. It was thought by the ancients that the sun, moon and planets were carried round, each by its own crystalline sphere set at fixed musical intervals apart and emitting a characteristic note. The sum of these notes was a "harmony", which, however, we mortals normally cannot hear since we have become habituated to it from birth.

CHAPTER 3

TACTILE EXPERIENCE

There were twelve examples. We find here just what we found with "voices" & "visions": the essence of the phenomenon is affective: a person may feel comforted, guided, reassured by a gentle pressure, or, more rarely, "punished" by a sharp blow. In short, the "touch" expresses an *affective* relation.

It may be felt on forehead, cheek, top of head, shoulder, arm ("just above the elbow"), or side —

(1) F m: ". . . Then something very strange and very wonderful happened, something that stays with me to this day. I felt pressure as if *someone* were touching me. There definitely was *pressure on my right side*. I felt lifted up. My whole being was filled with ecstasy... All cares were taken away — nothing of this world mattered. I knew there was another."

(2) M s 77 (Lt. Col.): "My daughter Joan was killed by a car when she was 7 years old. She and I were very close and I was grief-stricken. She was lying in her coffin in her bedroom. I fell on my knees by the bedside. Suddenly I felt as if something a bit *behind me* was so overcome with pity that it was consolidated itself. (I suppose that means 'taking shape'). Then I felt *a touch on my shoulder* lasting only an instant, and I knew there was another world . . ."

(3) F m: ". . . I was in a very weak state at home having lost 1½ stone in a fortnight's illness and my husband was at home suffering from great mental depression. After he had said he felt he couldn't go on any longer and I felt that I hadn't any strength to help him or myself, it seemed to me that my forehead was very swiftly *touched* and from that moment I took courage . . ."

(4) F m: ". . . very strong feeling that God *had his hand on my shoulder* and that of the man I later married . . ."

(5) F s: "One morning at the Incarnatus, I felt that *someone* was *pressing on my left shoulder*, and in obedience I knelt . . ."

(6) F m 69: "... I prayed ... and then I felt (and can feel it still when I think about it) a hand pressing on my right shoulder, and a voice said 'What are you worrying about, everything will be all right', and I felt such an inward peace ..."

A more powerful kind of pressure —

(7) F s (nun): "... I was praying in a relaxed position lying on my back in bed, and not thinking or saying much — just feeling round as it were and saying Jesus softly, gently, with pauses. Then I *felt a pressure* that was Christ's body pressed full length on mine so that I felt myself pressed further into the mattress. The closeness was as intimate and strong as intercourse — then, while remaining in full possession of my body, he went through into the very centre of my being. .."

A dead person's touch —

(8) F m 48: "When my mother died after a long illness, I felt that she was happy and contented ... After her funeral I returned to my home and for about six weeks I had the feeling that she was with me all the time, just being with me and watching the children and assuring herself that all went well with me and my family. After about six weeks I was lying in bed thinking about her and still feeling her presence strongly and always happily when I felt *an ice cold touch*[1] on my cheek. Just the lightest of touches but a cold I cannot describe. After that although I felt she was happy I never again had the feeling of her presence and it seemed to me that once she had 'lived' with me for some time and enjoyed being in my home she had touched me to say 'Goodbye'."

A guiding hand —

(9) F m 34: "... My particular story occurred when I was about 6 or 7 years old. I attended a Day Nursery at the time. One day I left the building to go home at the usual departure hour, but there was a terrible thunder and lightening storm just then, and although I was terrified I knew my mother expected me home and so ventured forth amongst the fallen trees, poles and electric wires. As I passed a doorway, on my right side, *I felt a hand firmly but gently on my left arm* just above the elbow and I was *guided* into this sheltered spot ..."

A more violent form of "guidance" —

(10) F m 50: "One day I went for a walk in a narrow valley in the hills. I was worried and perplexed and wished I was young again, and could ask a God whom I trusted whether the course of action I was tempted to follow would be wise. Suddenly a *whirlwind* came rushing down the valley, *caught me up* off the ground, *spun me round* several times and *threw me roughly down* with my face in the opposite direction."

"Punishment" —

(11) M s 31: ". . . In the spring of 1961, I was sitting up in bed recovering from emotional and physical exhaustion and was (shortly) afterwards treated for a somewhat acute, if short-lived, form of schizophrenia — paranoid and catatonic. While sitting up in bed, I decided to celebrate a little form of Communion though I was never formally ordained, and did not in the least consider this action in any way blasphemous. I thought it might bring some consolation as I was in an extreme period of mental torment. I used a small piece of ordinary bread and a little wine belonging to the landlady — dandelion I think it was. I crossed the bread as a Catholic priest does, before bending over it and pronouncing the words of consecration 'Hoc est enim corpus Deus'. I did the same with the wine and proceeded to communicate by breaking the bread and placing a piece of it in my mouth, washing it down with some wine. AT THAT MOMENT, I WAS *FORCIBLY STRUCK* BY AN INVISIBLE FORCE ON THE HEAD, IN THE REGION OF THE LEFT FRONTAL LOBE OF THE BRAIN . . ."

(12) F m 44: ". . . I got an impression on my right temple, like a voice saying . . . Turn your head to the right, and when I did, a *hard jolt* hit me right on the top of my head, like a bolt of lightning, it almost knocked me out . . ."

Five of the above — (1), (3), (6), (10) and (11) — were feeling anxious just before; one — (9) — was "terrified"; two — (2) and (8) — had been lately bereaved (but were in very different situations); five — (2), (5), (6), (7) and (11) — were praying at the time; one — (11) — was mentally ill.

It is striking that just "a touch" or "a pressure" was enough to suggest a divine presence, eliciting an immediate and powerful emotional response ("ecstasy . . . All cares were taken away". "I knew there was another world". "I took courage". "felt an inward peace", etc.).

Chapter 3: Notes

2. cf. the following examples: (from the second 1,000) "My mother died very suddenly in one room while I was having my first baby in the other room. After I had had the baby I was lying in bed alone and feeling so unhappy and thinking how dreadful life would be without my dear Mum when I felt a cold hand on my right shoulder and it squeezed and immediately it gave me renewed courage. I feel sure it was my mother's hand". (From the third 1,000) M w: ". . . On the morning of the funeral I felt strangely different, calm and collected, and viewed the whole proceedings in a detached sort of way, as if I was just a spectator at another's funeral, but inwardly I dreaded those last moments at the graveside. The service began and I held on very well without showing any signs of weakening, then the last prayer of committal and we all stood with closed eyes. Suddenly a hand gripped my left arm just between the elbow and shoulder, very firm and steadying. I immediately thought it was my brother-in-law, my wife's brother, and that he, anticipating my feelings, was giving me support. I remember thinking "How good of dear William to think of me at this terrible moment." I was held fast and reassured beyond measure. The prayer over, when we opened our eyes my brother-in-law was standing some ten feet away and no-one else was near touching me. Don't mistake, the grip was firm, almost pressing, not an accidental touch of a passer-by, and it continued until the prayer was over . . . From that day I have felt a different man . . . In touch with the Infinite, the Creator of Everything, just for a minute . . ."

CHAPTER 4

INWARD SENSATIONS

Several people mention vibrations or feelings of "electricity" in their bodies —

e.g. (1)   F m 51: "... A period of great longing for God and times of fear that I would lose him. I spent time on prayer and meditation. I had vibrations in my body ... And these seemed to be a confirmation to me that God was real and the *feeling of love and being loved* was deep ..."

This occurs especially in connection with healing or being healed —

(2)   F m 55 (priest): "We experience a warmth or vibration in our hands when we are to lay hands on people for healing or to receive the Spirit's annointing ..."

(3)   M m 58: (a research officer): "I was present purely from interest, having no physical need — so far as I knew — requiring healing ... As the priest laid his hands on my head and said a rather lovely prayer, I realised that his finger-tips contacting my scalp were becoming warmer and warmer. I felt an unusual heat in the tips of his fingers and then a type of vibration at the points of contact ... This description is factual. I do not understand it as my own fingers are normally the coldest parts of my body."

Feelings of "warmth" were common; they varied from peripheral sensations (as in (2) and (3) — *at the hands or finger-tips*) to "warmth of heart" —

(4)   F m: "All at once I *felt someone near me,* a Presence entered this little room of which I became immediately conscious. This feeling of second sense is a common one, and could be very frightening, but to me I was not afraid or alarmed ... Dazed I knelt by the nearest chair and here is the physical phenomenon that has recurred many times since. Into my heart there came a great *warmth.* The only way I can

113

describe it is in the words of disciples on their way to Emmaus 'our hearts burned within us'. My hand raised in prayer also glowed from tips to wrist with a blessed warmth and heat, never before experienced."

From the purely physical —

e.g. (5) F m: ". . . the preacher asked us to . . . pray and fast . . . This I did . . . and a few days later noticed that something had happened to me. I was a person who used to feel the cold, more than most people did; but ever since that fast I haven't felt the cold like I used to; it really is amazing how different I feel . . ."

to the more metaphorical (not that emotional warmth need exclude the physical) —

(6) F m 33: ". . . On Christmas Day early in the morning, I *felt* the presence of Almighty God which I had never experienced before. I was not confirmed, and had never received communion, but I needed him so desperately I was so terribly frightened — he came. It was a feeling — a strength that came to me as I lay in bed — holding tightly to the Bible. A *warmth* filled me — a sensation of peace engulfed me, and I was afraid no more . . ."

(7) M s 53: ". . . to my utter surprise I became aware of a personal presence with me. No voice, no vision, not even an 'inward heard' message. Simply the kind of *inward warmth* one has when one meets an old friend, and is aware of his affection and goodwill."

(8) M 77: ". . . As the sermon proceeded I gradually became diffused with a feeling of '*warmth*' which I hadn't ever experienced before and which made me feel that although the sermon evoked it, it came from higher source. The feeling seemed to be *almost visible* and seemed to be around me in a form extending from my head downwards . . ."

With this paradoxical "feeling of warmth" that "seemed to be *almost visible*", compare 1b (18): ". . . the room seemed all of a sudden filled with light . . . The curious thing is that I *felt the light*." In both cases, (and cf. Chapt.2, note 8), the mixture of seeing and feeling springs from a breakdown of the normal "inner"/"outer" dichotomy, the shortcomings of which we have already considered.

Several people described feelings of warmth that they experienced, surprisingly, upon bereavement —

(9) F m 46: ". . . Then, suddenly, my seventeen year old daughter took ill and after six agonising months of ups and downs, died. I remember at the end hoping she *would* die because I knew there would be irreparable brain damage had she not. My husband and I had been at the gates of Hell those months . . . yet strangely in the hospital cubicle in the minutes following her death, though she lay there a lovely seventeen year old cold and still, I felt a warmth. Just a warmth. It surprised me, I remember, though I said nothing to anyone at the time . . ."

(10) F m 57: "When I returned to the nursing home, three or four days later, after the death of my baby, I felt overwhelmed by grief and weakness. On the afternoon of the funeral, I was left alone in my room . . . As I waited, in the quiet house, I gradually became aware of a calmness and peace which completely took possession of me, and I felt this so strongly that, as my husband and others returned from the funeral, I felt that I could put my hand out and give it to them too. It was so positive, that it was as if someone had wrapped a warm cloak round me while standing shivering and naked in a storm . . ."

We have encountered so many cases of comforting "visions" (1a (21) — (23)), "lights" (1c (6) — (8) and "voices" (2a (13) — (19)) experienced by the newly bereaved, that feelings of "warmth" should not surprise us.

CHAPTER 5

THE SENSE OF PRESENCE

We have already encountered above, under "feelings of warmth", cases where somebody is "felt" to be there, even though nothing is seen or heard, and no touch is felt —

cf (4)   "I *felt* someone near me . . . there came a warmth."

(6)   ". . . I *felt* the presence of Almighty God . . . A warmth filled me."

(7)   "I became aware of a personal presence. No voice, no vision . . . Simply the kind of inward warmth one has when one meets an old friend, and is aware of his affection and good will."

How can one "feel" a "presence" without perceiving anything? By its emotional effects, evidently[1]. Here, warmth[2], but in other cases, where the "presence" is disturbing not comforting, by feelings of shame or fear. There is always an *effective* personal relation, prior to any objective perception.

The small child has a feeling of incompleteness when left alone by someone he needs (even though he may be too young to be aware of their separate existence), so their return, and presence, gives him a feeling of warmth, of being loved; and he may even have the feeling without any sensory manifestation of their presence.

In our accounts too there is emotional dependence. There is always this affective personal relationship implied. One never gets this sort of account of a sense of presence — "I suddenly felt a presence in the room. I felt that this presence was unaware of me. Its attention was elsewhere" — just as one never gets — "I felt a touch. This seemed to be a presence brushing past on its way elsewhere" — or — "I heard a voice. It was the voice of God addressing somebody else". The presence is felt to exist (like the small child's parent) only in relation to oneself, as the cause of an emotional effect on one. Nor do you get people saying "I had this sudden feeling of a presence in the room" with reference to some inanimate object, like a table or a chair. At the other end of the relation you never get anyone saying "I felt this benign presence. I ignored it" — or — "I had other things to do" — or — "It had no effect on me". The two things — feeling of "presence" and emotional "response" to it — are tied indissolubly. To experience it is to react to it. One cannot (e.g.) sense a benign presence without feeling comforted by it, or a disapproving one without feeling shame.

Why not? Because if I am emotionally dependent on someone, then my attitude towards myself mirrors what I take to be their attitude towards me. They disapprove. I disapprove of myself (feel ashamed); they admire me, I admire myself (exult); they show me affection, I feel friendly towards myself ("warm"). In psychoanalytic jargon, I "identify" myself with their attitude towards me. Now it would be odd for someone to say of his feelings towards himself "I was very annoyed with myself (e.g. for forgetting an appointment), but I shrugged my annoyance aside contemptuously". And it is for this reason that it would be equally odd if someone said "I felt this wrathful presence. I ignored it". Attitude to self and attitude shown to one by a feared and needed Other are not to be separated.

We take for granted the way a child learns to talk by echoing the sounds his parents make, and in general the way he mimics their actions and mannerisms. Less obvious, but more fundamental from our point of view, is the way his mimicry involuntarily makes him adopt towards himself the attitudes they display towards him. An adult (if emotionally mature) can take a step back, and compare and contrast his own point of view with that of other people, in particular he can compare his view of himself with their view of him; but we are not born with this objectivity, this sense of our own identity as something separate from and independent of the Other; the child's emotional needs make him "live" the Other's attitude towards him (except when he rebels), and feel towards himself, as opposed to understanding, what the Other feels towards him. He cannot distinguish what he really is from what others think of him.

This tendency to "become" the Other, latent in dependent

117

relations, becomes manifest in the following examples. In fantasy, when for example we imagine making some deliciously witty remark, or rehearse an angry confrontation with our employer, we seem to play both parts, to "live" both ends of the relation — we are speaker and admiring (or discomforted) other party in one. In dreams, we sometimes see someone from the outside and yet at the same time seem to "experience" their feelings as though we were inside their skin. In real life, in moments of anxiety or excitement, the same thing may happen without our noticing, as when watching a tottering acrobat, we make desperate efforts to keep "his" balance, or, watching our putt agonisingly slow up before it reaches the hole, we make little effortful movements as though we *were* the ball. (The connection with strong emotion is a vital one, for this is what "projects" us beyond ourselves.) Also, we may recall those explicit accounts of feelings of "oneness" (1d above), where, in a trance, the individual momentarily loses all sense of time, space and separate identity, and feels himself "merge" with a leaf, a buzzard, a tree, or the whole of nature.

I quoted this account earlier (1e (26) above):

> "That first night in the ward, one of the nuns knelt down and said the following:
>
> 'Be present, O merciful Lord, and protect us through the silent hours of this night so that we, who are wearied by the changes and chances of this fleeting world may repose upon Thy Eternal Changelessness'.
>
> For the first time, a great peace fell on me; and it seemed to me that 'I' was looking down with infinitely tender pity upon this pathetic, crushed, disfigured N (herself); and in that moment of realisation I knew I was no longer identified with her, but was on some entirely different level of consciousness. With the utmost conviction, I knew that I was a soul looking at its vehicle the temporary personality."

— and I pointed out that not only was she no longer "identified" with her own body, as she says, but she was "identifying" herself with the merciful figure who is being addressed (as child does with parent). This is the sort of "identifying" I have in mind in saying the dependent child involuntarily adopts towards himself what he feels to be the parent's attitude towards him. But, you may reply, there is this great difference: — the parent is physically there to be imitated; but in our example there is no such physical presence — she is "identifying" with empty air. So we come to the next point: the child not only "introjects" the parent's attitudes towards him (re-enacts them towards himself), but he also foists them on to more or less appropriate others, whom he then sees (according to mood and context) as friendly or disapproving "parent-figures" — like the self-conscious person who, because he feels ridiculous himself, imagines everyone is looking at him, laughing at him, when probably no one has even noticed him.

Anything may be a peg on which to hang a "projection" (cf. 1a (11) — (14): portraits, statues, wallpaper) or there may be *no need of a physical peg at all,* as with the small child's "imaginary companion" — not so different from the grown-up's feeling of a "presence"[3].

Can we throw any light on this phenomenon of "projection"? It is in origin the other half of what we have just discussed — the child's tendency to "become" the other person. Instead of (or as well as) incorporating the other's attitudes, he may unconsciously invest the other with his own. There is a confusion between me and the other, a sort of bodily overlap or exchange, so that I not only seem to "feel" the other's gestures and expression as though they were my own — the "outside" that I see becomes the "inside" that I feel — but (the other side of the same coin) the "inside" that I feel may become the "outside" that I see[4]; as with the self-conscious person who wrongly feels everyone is laughing at him. Again, some related examples may make this clear. In dreams, I not only seem at times to feel the other person's feelings "from the inside", but sometimes it seems as if I am looking at myself from the outside, as though I were another person. We had two examples earlier of a similar sort of "reversal" in waking life (1a (18) and (19) above), where "Quite suddenly it seemed that I was being looked at, and the look seemed to come from the tree", and "It was as if I and the tree had changed places . . . I was the object and the tree had become the subject". And we had many cases (1e above) where people felt

119

briefly as if they were looking at themselves from outside their own bodies. More generally (1f above) we saw how a change in one's own mood could effect a transformation in what one sees around one; in extreme excitement, what one sees may even become alive and animated like oneself (cf. 1d (21) and 2d (2) above); — compare the small child's tendency to treat an inanimate thing as if it were a "you" (another "me") alive and with feelings like (or complementary to) his own at that moment. And not just the small child: the impatient adult may swear at the "obstinate" knot in his shoelace, or kick the chair he has just tripped over[5].

So one may see and respond to another person, a thing or even a void, as if they felt towards one's own feelings (or their complement) — i.e. unconsciously construct them in one's own image, as a reflection of oneself (or part of oneself).

To return to the sense of "presence". There were 113 accounts of it in the first thousand letters. Now for some examples —

(1)   M 77 (somebody in the trenches under fire for the first time): "As man after man went down, however, a Presence came to me which took away all my fears and replaced them with a feeling of ecstasy."

(2)   F m 40 (as a child picking flowers in a field near Truro): "Suddenly I felt myself overwhelmed by a presence which kept me standing still in the middle of the field, and later I described it to myself as 'the whole world seemed to stand still'."

(3)   M 38: "The whole room seemed to be filled by an overwhelming Presence, and I was filled with an absolute peace. I even looked up at the empty place beside my chair, seeing nothing, but aware that all was well . . ."

(4)   F m 61: "I remember my first consciousness of God as a loving presence when, as quite a small child, I found myself alone in a wood; it was still and peaceful, and God was there and that was enough."

(5)   F m 47: "Since my very early childhood, 4 or 5, I had the feeling of a Presence. This Presence was of great comfort always, especially as I suffered from asthma and the feeling of this Presence always had a very good effect."

(6) F m 39: "When I was quite ill with the unromantic complaint of mumps I had a remarkable experience of the presence of the power of Jesus and really felt forgiveness."

(7) F m 55: "This power beyond my own ego is not altogether beyond it or separate from it. It is as personal and 'of me' as the colour of my eyes, it is friendly and reliable, resourceful and companionable."

(8) M 42: "I met with a very severe accident at work . . . at times the pain was excruciating; and yet, unmistakably, I felt a very real presence at my side as if someone was sharing the pain with me."

(9) F m 35: "Although the room was dark and I was alone, I had an overwhelming feeling that I was not alone. Someone was there with me. So near that this presence seemed to completely enfold me. I was not afraid but very awed. It was a comforting presence, and almost as suddenly as I had time to realise this, it quickly departed, and I knew I was alone again."

(10) M 24: "Particularly in the countryside, I am overwhelmed by the feeling that something all-powerful and merciful and sympathetic is very close, so close that communication by prayer is imperative — I want to speak and can speak to that something and it understands my needs and desires . . ."

(11) F m 60: "Then, just as I was exhausted and despairing — I had the most wonderful sense of the presence of God. He was in a particular place in the room about five feet from me — I didn't look up, but kept my head in my hands and my eyes shut. It was a feeling of an all-embracing love which called forth every ounce of love I had in me. It was the tenderest love I have ever encountered and my sins were blotted out completely."

(12) M 63: "At the height of the panic, when I didn't know what to do, I was conscious of, not a voice or a presence in recognizable form, but a live certainty as if there was an 'I' 'present' outside me and yet directed at me personally."

(13) F m 44: "I was walking along a long, lonely country road by myself; worried sick and in near despair. Then came the experience. It lasted about 20 minutes — I sensed a

presence, on my right, keeping level with me as I went along. A mental message was conveyed in my mind; the sense of it being: 'Don't worry; it will all turn out all right.' It was not the message that counted so much as the overwhelming sense of infinite understanding, compassion and sympathy."

(14) F m 38: "It was as though an outside personality had seized me and entered inside to fill up my skin to bursting point."

(15) F m 55: "I am not at all an energetic or well-organized person, I have very little will power to tackle the problems and tasks of every day ... Then inside myself, I say: 'Please, You help me to start, Where must I begin?' And somehow it is as if someone took me by the hand, the way we do it for blind people so that they can orientate themselves — I am set in motion ... Of course, one may say that 'prayers' of the above kind do nothing else than summon some energy within ourselves. But why should we then feel so helpless without it, or so grateful when we have received it?"

(16) M 68: "I was deeply distressed ... One evening I was sitting in a chair in our small study in the dark and I was conscious of a Person in the room just as you know when anyone else enters a room by their personality . . . I felt a golden, glorious feeling of love."

(17) M 71: "Then, in a very gentle and gradual way, not with a shock at all, it began to dawn on me that I was not alone in the room. Someone else was there, located fairly precisely about two yards to my right front. Yet there was no sort of sensory hallucination. I neither saw him nor heard him in any sense of the word 'see' and 'hear', but there he was and I had no doubt about it. He seemed to be very good and very wise, full of sympathetic understanding, and most kindly disposed towards me."

(18) M 60: "There was no sensible vision, but the room was filled by a Presence which in a strange way was both about me and within me. I was overwhelmingly possessed by Someone who was not myself, and yet I felt I was more myself than I had ever been before . . ."

First, location of the "presence": some people say "I felt a presence was beside me" — cf. (3) and (8); some are even more particular — "It was just five feet away", or something like that — cf. (11) and (17); others talk about an "inner presence" — cf. (7) and (14); or a "presence" "both about me and within me" — (18).

Next, what was their mood immediately before, and what were the circumstances? Panic (12); fear under fire (1); illness or pain (5), (6) and (8); exhaustion, despair (11); near despair, worried sick (13); helpless (15); deeply distressed (10).

What was the attitude of the "presence" towards them? "Loving" (4); "friendly and reliable" (7); "sharing the pain" (8); "comforting" (9); "all-powerful, merciful and sympathetic" (10); "all-embracing love" (11); "infinite understanding, compassion and sympathy" (13); "full of sympathetic understanding, and most kindly disposed towards me" (17).

And what effect did it have on them? "All was well" (3); "of great comfort", "very good effect" (5); "felt forgiveness" (6); "not afraid but very awed", "comforting" (9); "my sins were blotted out completely" (11); "I am set in motion", "grateful" (15); "feeling of love" (16); "I was overwhelmingly possessed by Someone who was not myself, and yet I felt I was more myself than I had ever been before" (18)[6].

What do we learn in general from these examples? That when I feel a "presence", it is as if the Other is present *to me* personally, existing (from my point of view) only in relation to me. I feel the "presence" of the Other-as-subject, for whom I am object (this is the essence of the dependent relation); I am the object of his feelings, as it seems to me, I am on the "receiving end"[7]; I have a sense of *"being looked at"*; I respond emotionally, I am not just an observer; the Other is my "You" in an immediate, dependent relation. I may feel I am being looked at lovingly[8], warmly (as in most of these examples), or wrathfully, malignantly, or whatever; and my feeling of being looked at in these ways *is* my feeling of sudden warmth, comfort, support, or shame, terror, embarrassment or whatever. I relax, uncoil, expand; or I blush, tremble, sink to my knees. These "reactive" sensations are just what conveys to me the immediate "presence" of the friendly or hostile) Other; they *are* my sense of the Other's "presence" —

blushing *is* the feeling of being exposed to the Other's look (whether or not he is really looking at me).

According to Sartre, *"being-seen-by-the Other* is the truth of seeing-the-Other", and this is at least true of the dependent relationship. "Through shame we confer on the Other an *indubitable* presence", even when "it is only probable that the Other is looking at me". "Although I immediately experience and with certainty the fact of being-looked-at, I cannot make this certainty pass into my experience of the Other-as-*object*. In fact it only reveals to me the Other-as-subject, a transcending presence to the world and the real condition of *my* being-as-object". In "mystic experiences of the presence of the Other", God is "the omnipresent, infinite subject for whom I exist", "the infinite subject which is never an object", "the Being who looks at us and can never be looked at". Now my "being looked-at . . . . . is not in itself bound to the Other's *body* . . . It is never eyes which look at us; it is the Other-as-subject . . . who is present to me *without distance*". "The Other's presence remains *undifferentiated*"[9]; — small wonder that many accounts are ambiguous as to whether the "presence" they experienced was "within" or "without" (just as we saw with accounts of "light" and "voices" above), and that a sense of presence requires no visible manifestation.

For many, the "presence" was not that of a god, but of someone very close to them who had died[10]. Even (physical) absence is not felt to be incompatible with (spiritual) "presence"; absence is itself a relation between persons —
cf. Donne:

> His mind hath found
> Affection's ground
> Beyond time, place and all mortality:
> To hearts that cannot vary
> *Absence is presence,* time doth tarry.

and St. Matthew 28:20:

> "Lo, I am with you always, even unto the end of the world".

St. Teresa, like Sartre, stresses the indubitable certainty of the sense of presence:

> "One day when I was at prayer . . . I saw Christ at my side —
> or, to put it better, I sensed Him, for I saw nothing with the
> eyes of the body or the eyes of the soul I felt that He was
> quite close to me . . . I was at first very much *afraid* and did
> nothing but weep. What I felt very clearly was that all the
> time He was at my right hand, a *witness of everything that I
> was doing*" (cf. "Other-as-subject" above). "If I say I do not
> see Him with the eyes of the body or the eyes of the soul,
> because this is no vision with images, how then can I know
> and affirm that He is beside me with *greater certainty than if
> I saw Him*? If one says that one is like someone in the dark
> who cannot see another though he is beside Him, or like
> someone who is blind, this is not a fair comparison. There is
> some similarity, but not much, because the person in the
> dark can perceive the other with his other senses, hear him
> speak or move, or touch him. Here this is not so, nor is there
> any feeling of darkness — on the contrary, He manifests His
> presence to the soul by a knowledge brighter than the sun . . .
> The Lord is pleased to engrave it so deeply on the
> understanding that one can no more doubt it than one can
> doubt the evidence of one's eyes. In fact *it is easier to doubt
> one's eyes*. For sometimes we wonder whether we have not
> imagined what we see, whereas here, though that suspicion
> may arise for a moment, there remains such complete
> *certainty* that the doubt has no force."

Many of our own accounts make the same point —

e.g. (19) F m: "The Holy Spirit has been my constant companion —
> though I am the chief of sinners — *and I am more certain of
> his presence than I am of any material fact.*"

(20) F m 60: ". . . in that moment, I *knew* God and *have known
> him* ever since . . ."

(21) M 45: ". . . For my part, these feelings of coming together
> with some great force are very real; there is nothing fragile
> about these experiences; they are *as positive as breathing* . . ."

and from the above cf.

(12) ". . . not a voice or a presence in recognizable form but — a
> *live certainty* as if there was an 'I' present . . ."

(17) "... I neither saw him nor heard him in any sense of the word 'see' and 'hear' but there he was and *I had no doubt about it* ..."

Chapter 5: Notes

1. cf. St. Teresa: "The soul recognizes the presence of God by the *effects* He produces on the soul, for that is the way He is pleased to make His presence *felt*."

2. cf. Henry James, *The Golden Bowl*: ". . . There was a little dry patch in her heart that seemed to cry out for the warm summer rain that only *his presence* could give."

3. cf. F m 68: "When my youngest son was *about two* (that is nearly 24 years ago) there appeared to be a strange unseen presence in the house. It seemed to attach itself to my youngest son and me. But *mostly to my son* . . . in fact, it was he who nicknamed this attachment 'Charlie' . . . When my son went away to College . . . it left the house . . . When my son and I had the row and he left home in August '68, this attachment went for about four weeks, then came back and has remained ever since. It has saved me from quite a few very serious accidents. Also it gives me warning of anything evil surrounding me . . .".

4. Or hear — Thus one contributor writes of an absent friend: ". . . While lying on my bed . . . I could hear her voice *in my throat*" (Chapt. 2, note 8); and cf. Gould, *American Journal of Psychiatry*, 1950: observation of 84 patients revealed involuntary movements of *their own* speech organs while they were hearing "voices".

5. Poets are particularly prone to animism in their writings. Ruskin called this the "pathetic" fallacy, and emphasised its close connection with emotion, noting "the difference between the ordinary, proper and true appearances of things to us and the extraordinary, or false appearances, when we are *under the influence of* emotion; false appearances, I say, as being entirely unconnected with any real power or character in the object, and only *imputed* to it by us". The pathetic fallacy is "a fallacy caused by the excited state of the feelings, making us, for the time, more or less irrational". The error is one "which the mind admits *when affected strongly by emotion*. Thus, for instance, in *Alton Locke*

   They rowed her across the rolling foam —
   The cruel, crawling foam.

   The foam is not cruel, neither does it crawl. The state of mind which attributes to it these characteristics of a living creature is one in which reason is unhinged by grief. All *violent feelings* have the same effect. They produce in us a falseness in all our impressions of external things, which I would generally characterise as the "Pathetic Fallacy'." Ruskin goes on to contrast genuine with forced examples of this fallacy: "Now so long as the *feeling* is *true*, we pardon, or are even pleased by, the confessed fallacy of sight which it induces: we are pleased, for instance, with those lines of Kingsley's above quoted not because they fallaciously describe foam, but because they faithfully describe sorrow. But the moment the mind of the speaker becomes *cold*, that moment every such expression becomes untrue, as being forever untrue in the external facts."

6. R. D. Laing (op.cit.) perhaps throws light on this paradox, connecting presence of needed other with heightened sense of own identity: ". . . The mother, however, is not simply a *thing* which the child can see, but a *person* who sees the child. Therefore, we suggest that a necessary component in the development of the self is the *experience of oneself as a person under the loving eye of the mother*". (p. 116); ". . . the . . . other in whose eyes he lived and moved and had his being". (p. 117); (of a female patient) — "Although she was by herself at home, she was always able to have someone with her *in a magical way*". "If she is not in the actual presence of another person who knows her, or if she cannot succeed in *invoking this person's presence in his absence*, her sense of her own identity drains away from her . . . For her, *esse* is *percipi*".

7. cf. Buber: "We receive what we did not hitherto have, and we receive it in such a way that we know it has been given us."

8. cf. Numbers 7: 25-6: "The Lord make his face to shine upon thee. . . . The Lord life up the Light of his countenance upon thee . . ."; also Psalms 31: 16, 67:1, 80:3, 7:19 and 4:6.

9. Sartre, *L'Etre et le Néant,* part 2.

10. cf. *Hallucinations of Widowhood* by Dr. W. D. Rees, cited Chapt. 1, note 8 above.

CHAPTER SIX

CONCLUSION

These various kinds of experience, except for 1d-f, are essentially personal: you feel the voice or presence or whatever as a second person, a "you"; and you experience the Other purely in relation to yourself, as comforting, benevolent, malignant or whatever; it is an affective relation, and the response is an emotional one, — warmth, a feeling of being loved, shame, awe, and so on. What I think might be true to say is this: the sense of presence, the sense that somebody is "there" without any sensory manifestations, seems to be if anything the primary thing, and the rest (voice, vision, etc.) comes as a sensory elaboration of it. Take, for instance, those cases of being touched — if I felt a light pressure on my arm, I don't think I would infer from that, unless under very particular circumstances, that this was anything benevolent or punishing, that it was a "presence", a Being of some kind; it would just be rather an odd nervous sensation. I think the feeling of somebody being near, of their having a certain *attitude* towards you, is the basic thing, from which the rest follows.

After all, if we add to the sense of "presence" a "voice", "appearance", "touch" or whatever, nothing crucially different results; the "presence" is simply filled out for us. It makes no great difference whether the Other looks at me, speaks to me, touches me, or I simply sense his "presence", these are just so many ways of expressing an effective relation, and that is the primary thing.

Consider the following —

> "Then suddenly Mole felt a great awe fall upon him, an awe that turned his muscles to water, bowed his head . . . Without seeing, he *knew it could only mean* that some august presence was very, very near."
>
> (Kenneth Grahame, *The Wind in the Willows*)

Ruskin similarly writes of —

> ". . . an instinctive awe, mixed with delight, an indefinable thrill, such as we sometimes *imagine to indicate* the presence of a disembodied spirit."

But how can this be? Normally we know there is someone present just because we can see them, hear them, etc.

> "It is as if" says William James, "there were in the human consciousness a sense of reality, a feeling of objective presence, a perception of what we may call 'something there' more deep and more general than any of the special and particular 'senses' by which the current psychology supposes existent realities to be originally revealed."

And he suggests an analogy:

> "It is as if a bar of iron, without touch or sight, with no representative faculty whatever, might nevertheless be strongly endowed with an inner capacity for magnetic feeling and as if, through the various arousals of its magnetism by magnets coming and going in its neighbourhood, it might be consciously determined to different attitudes and tendencies. Such a bar or iron could never give you an outward description of the agencies that had the power of stirring it so strongly; yet of their presence, and of their significance for its life, it would be intensely aware through every fibre of its being."[1]

Note the words "feeling", "arousals", "attitudes", "significance for its life". We are not born into the world as dispassionate observers of phenomena, but as organisms striving to satisfy certain vital needs. Piaget's observations show that for the young child "objects" exist only in relation to himself, as the poles of possible actions — to be sucked, to be grasped, to be avoided, or whatever. The object is "tied" to the particular action, so that the one cannot occur without the other. To recognise an object is to respond to it appropriately. The child's response "forms", as it were, the object for him, giving it its meaning for him.

Now, suppose not an object but a person, on whom the child depends, and to whose presence he responds, say, with a mixture of love and fear. Then the meaning of this Other for him will be something like "to be bowed down to", and the awareness of his presence will be the experiencing of the feelings of warmth, awe, etc., that it inspires, as opposed to the feeling of incompleteness in his absence.

But just as this Other cannot be near without arousing the corresponding feelings, the appropriate response, in him, (like the magnet and the sentient bar of iron), so, if these same feelings should happen to recur in the Other's absence, they may give rise to a more or less vivid image of him, or sense of his "presence", as their invariable author.

But why should they ever recur in the Other's absence, if they are "tied" to his presence? To understand this we must understand the force of *need*, in helping to form what we perceive or imagine[2]. When I need something, or am searching for something, I carry before me an image of it in my mind. Which is to say, as objects are poles of action, I already incipiently go through the motions of the particular action corresponding to it; so the image is formed, springing from my expectant or wishful feelings, and anticipating the object itself. And so, when I am looking for something, I tend to notice it, or things like it, rather than other kinds of things; for I have already partly "formed" it for myself (the behaviourist would talk of "fractional responses" and "reduced thresholds of recognition").

In intense need, this image, or imagined "presence", may take on the affective force of reality — i.e. elicit the full response to which it is tied. Von Uexkull describes how a young starling, brought up in a room without having a chance to see a fly, let alone catch one, one day was seen to rush towards an invisible "object", catch it in mid-air, return with it to its perch, peck away at it with its bill as any starling will do with a captured fly, and finally swallow the invisible thing. Evidently the starling's whole world was so charged with the need to feed that, even without the appearance of a sensory stimulus, it went through all the motions of the instinctive response on an imaginary fly.

Similarly Freud suggests that the hungry infant hallucinates the mother's breast, when he goes through the motions of sucking by himself. (Piaget observes how often the child goes through the appropriate motions in the absence of the object "tied" to them, instead of looking for the object). The adult too, according to Freud, dreams and mistakes for real, images that derive "full sensory vividness" from the force of the repressed infantile *wishes* that give rise to them. And in his studies of hysteria he found that "if one succeeds in bringing to consciousness infantile scenes . . . they appear as hallucinations" because of the strength of the repressed *feelings* attaching to them. Writing of bereavement, he says, "Reality-testing has shown that the loved object no longer exists, and it proceeds to demand that all libido shall be withdrawn from its attachments to that object. This demand arouses understandable opposition — it is a matter of general observation that people never willingly abandon a libidinal position, not even, indeed, when a substitute is already beckoning to them. This opposition can be so intense that a turning away from reality takes place and *a clinging to the object through the medium of a hallucinatory wishful psychosis*[3]." I have already cited W. D. Rees' survey, *Hallucinations of Widowhood*[4]. P. Marris[5], who interviewed seventy-two widows, aged between 25 and 56, at some point during the two years after they had lost their husbands, found that as many as half of them had experienced after their husband's death a sense of his continuing presence.

The anticipatory image that guides our search is well described by William James, here in the context of trying to recall a forgotten name:

> ". . . The state of our consciousness is peculiar. There is a gap therein; but no mere gap. It is a sort of gap that is intensely *active*. A sort of *wraith* of the name is in it, *beckoning us* in a given direction, making us at moments tingle with the sense of our closeness, and then letting us sink back without the longed-for term. If wrong names are proposed to us, this singularly definite gap acts immediately so as to negate them. They do not fit into its *mould*[6]."

The name is "longed for". Affect (our incipient, would-be response) gives us a "wraith" or vague image of it; reality (our full response, the utterance of the name) will fill it out, objectify it.

It is our affect that forms the image, not vice versa. As Sartre says, "It is my love of Annie that causes the image of her face to appear before me, and not the image of her face that excites a glow of love for her". And Proust clearly realises this when he writes of a particular kind of dream in which —

> "Just as Eve was created from a rib of Adam, so a woman would come into existence while I was sleeping, conceived from some strain in the position of my limbs. *Formed by the appetite that I was on the point of gratifying,* she it was, I imagined, who offered me that gratification. My body, conscious that its own warmth was permeating hers, would strive to become one with her, and I would awake. The rest of humanity seemed very remote in comparison with this woman whose company I had left but a moment ago; my cheek was still warm with her kiss, my body bent beneath the weight of hers . . ."[7]

We have seen how, formed and made vivid by the presence of intense need, we may be led to treat the "image", "wraith" or "outline" as real; that is, to respond in full when the object of our feelings is not really there. But this response is not necessarily tied to a full-blown sensory image of the Other. Whether we "realise" the (e.g.) comforting Other visually, through hearing, or through touch, or simple as an intangible "presence", the essential thing is the *effect* it is felt to have on us, the change in our feelings from despair to joy and love. This effect is our response. We do not even need a sense of the Other's actual "presence" in order to feel it, as can be seen from the everyday phenomena of faith and prayer — less dramatic but perhaps more truly remarkable than the vivid episodes we have been concerned with[8]. In (15) above, there is not literally a sense of "presence". Having prayed ("Please, you help me to start"), then "It is *as if* I am taken by the hand . . .". What matters is "I am set in motion", no longer "helpless". St. Teresa writes "It is *as if,* when we are on the point of praying, we seem to find Him whom we are about to address, and we seem to know that He is bearing us by the spiritual feeling and *effects* of great love and faith of which we become conscious."

One of our contributors writes —

> "In times of distress I have often found my own pleas or

133

prayers answered, sometimes by an inexplicable feeling of peace which seems to arise simply from the fact of praying — although *I do not know who or what I am praying to.*"

Another —

"From time to time a sense of stillness . . . in my kitchen as I worked I was in a worshipping state *without any clear image of a person to worship.*"

— (cf. *The Cloud of Unknowing* — "He may well be loved but not thought. By love may be begotten and holden; but by thought never.")

A third contributor goes even further —

". . . This power is more or less constant, but there are times when it is replaced by a vague feeling of uneasiness, a tendency to worry unnecessarily, or a failure to look for priorities. I think of it as faith; not faith in God, but faith which *is* God."

In sum, what impresses us most about these accounts? First, one is struck by the dependent, personal (I-You) basis of the experiences. If one chooses to talk of hallucinations, then these are not the experiencing of hallucinatory sensations (particular colours, sounds, etc.) but of hallucinatory meetings; "person", not "sensation", is the basic element; more often than not there is an inter-sensory overlap — e.g. something, or rather someone, is not only "seen", but "heard" or "touched" as well, or else they are felt to be "there" just as surely without any sensory evidence at all.

Next, strong emotion tends to colour not only the experience itself and its effect, but also the situation leading up to it. Very often the experience brings a sudden dramatic reversal of feeling — e.g. from the depths of despair to unbounded joy.

Then there is the point that, while some contributors locate the "voice", "light", "presence" or whatever in the outside world, others say it is "within", while still others say it is both at once, — cf. (18) above: ". . . a Presence which in a strange way was both about me and within me". This seems to be symptomatic of a general indistinctness between "inner" and "outer", "self" and "other", active and passive (i.e. whether I am doing it or it is being done to me) that may occur in moments of high excitement. Thus with "voices", one contributor felt he was being addressed by the voice of another that nevertheless "seemed to come from inside myself" (2b (9) above).

The "meeting", then, is no ordinary sort of meeting. The "You" may be (to quote from the Upanishads) "both without us and within us"; "closer is he than breathing, nearer than hands or feet". An English philosopher, F. H. Bradley, writes ". . . the reality of God means his actual presence within individual souls, and apart from this presence both he and they are no more than abstractions". Buber puts it more simply "In the beginning is relation . . . There is no 'I' taken by myself, but only the 'I' of the primary word 'I-You' ". If 'You' is said, the 'I' of 'I-You' is said with it".

Chapter 6: Notes

1. *The Varieties of Religious Experience.*

2. The same can be said of the force of expectancy, or suggestion, as is most dramatically demonstrated by the hynotist. His subject, with critical faculties lulled in a trance, is told that when he comes round he will not see X (who is really present) or will see Y (who is not); that if he plunges his arm into a bowl of water he will find it scalding (when in fact it is ice cold); that when a needle is passed through his cheek he will feel no pain, and so on. And sure enough, he does not see X, though X is standing in front of him; but he does say he sees the absent Y. When he takes his arm from the icy water, it is blistered as if by great heat; and then pierced by the needle, he feels nothing. All this because he sees and feels only what he has been led to expect. His own contribution to what he perceives (an essential one) is in this case determined by the influence of another's words.

3. *Mourning and Melancholia,* Hogarth Press, 1957, p. 244.

4. See p. 13 above.

5. *Widows and Their Families,* P. Marris, R.K.P., 1958.

6. *The Varieties of Religious Experience.*

7. *Swann's Way.*

8. "I remember the ways of life of many unknown and humble people whom I have met and respected. It seems to me that these people have done, effectively and consistently, many things which all ordinary sources of evidence seem to set outside the range of unassisted humanity. When they say 'It is God working through me' I cannot see that I have either the right or the knowledge to reject their testimony." Professor F. C. Bartlett.

Printed by **ZiPrint** Parchment (Oxford) Ltd., 60 Hurst Street, Oxford